How To Use Companies To Reduce Property Taxes

By

Lee Sharpe

Publisher Details
This guide is published by Tax Portal Ltd. 3 Sanderson Close, Great Sankey, Warrington, Cheshire, WA5 3LN.

How To Use Companies To Reduce Property Taxes– First published as '**Tax DOs and DON'Ts for Property Companies**' in May 2008, Second Edition May 2009. Third Edition August 2010. Fourth Edition May 2011. Fifth Edition April 2012. Sixth Edition May 2013. Seventh Edition April 2014. Eighth Edition April 2015. Ninth Edition April 2016. Tenth Edition April 2017 Eleventh Edition April 2018.

Publisher Details

This guide is published by Tax Portal Ltd., 3 Sandstone Close, Great Sankey, Warrington, Cheshire, WA5 3LN

How To Use Companies To Reduce Property Taxes. First published as "Tax DOs and DON'Ts for Property Companies" in May 2008. Second Edition May 2009. Third Edition August 2010. Fourth Edition May 2011. Fifth Edition April 2012. Sixth Edition May 2013. Seventh Edition April 2014. Eighth Edition April 2015. Ninth Edition April 2016. Tenth Edition April 2017. Eleventh Edition April 2018

Contents

About Lee Sharpe..9

About This Guide...10

1.   Choosing the Right Structure...12
   1.1.   Sole Trader...12
   1.2.   Partnership..12
   1.3.   Limited Company...12
   1.4.   Types of Partnerships..12
      1.4.1.   A "Limited Partnership"...13
      1.4.2.   A Limited Liability Partnership (known as an LLP)........14

2.   Getting to Grips with Limited Companies...................................15
   2.1.   The Different Types of Limited Company..............................15
   2.2.   The Basic Rules for a Company...15

3.   Understanding Corporation Tax...18
   3.1.   The Rates of Corporation Tax...18
   3.2.   Key Dates for the Company..18
   3.3.   Benefiting from the Favourable Company Taxes....................19
   3.4.   Extracting the Cash from the Company................................19
      3.4.1.   Paying a Salary...20
      3.4.2.   Paying Dividends...21
      3.4.3.   Paying Dividends and a Salary.................................23

4.   Building Up a Property Portfolio Using a Company.......................26
   4.1.   Using a Company to Grow Your Property Portfolio.................26

5.   Disallowance of Mortgage Interest on Residential Properties........28

6.   Everything You Need to Know About Dividend Payments...............30
   6.1.   Working with "Distributable Profits"....................................30
   6.2.   Who Gets the Dividends?...31
   6.3.   The Two Types of Dividend...31
      6.3.1.   A "Final" Dividend..32
      6.3.2.   An "Interim" Dividend...32
   6.4.   Getting the Paperwork Right...32
      6.4.1.   Sample – Meeting Minute..32
      6.4.2.   Sample – Dividend Confirmation...............................34
   6.5.   Two Pitfalls to Avoid when Making Dividend Payments...........35
      6.5.1.   Illegal Dividends...35
      6.5.2.   Timing of Dividends...35
   6.6.   Using Dividend Waivers – An Effective Tax Planning Tool........35
   6.7.   Watch out for the "Settlements" Legislation.........................36

7.   The Property Development Company **38**

7.1.   *The Property Developer* *38*

7.2.   *Companies and Property Developers* *38*

7.3.   *The Construction Industry Scheme ("CIS")* *41*

8.   Incorporation Relief **42**

8.1.   *Transferring Assets into Your Company* *42*
    8.1.1.   Holdover Relief for Gifts of Business Assets 42
    8.1.2.   Incorporation in Exchange for Shares 44

8.2.   *Watch Out for Three Pitfalls* *45*
    8.2.1.   "Preordained Series of Transactions" 45
    8.2.2.   Stamp Duty Land Tax 45
    8.2.3.   What is a "Business"? 45

8.3.   *Incorporating an Existing Property Investment Portfolio* *47*

9.   Entrepreneurs' Relief ("ER") from CGT **48**

10.   Reinvestment Relief **49**

10.1.   *Property Investors and Reinvestment Relief* *49*
    10.1.1.   Business Assets 49
    10.1.2.   Furnished Holiday Lettings 49

10.2.   *Deferring Capital Gains by Reinvesting* *51*
    10.2.1.   Enterprise Investment Scheme (EIS) 51

11.   Some Property Tax Pitfalls **54**

11.1.   *Partnerships?* *54*
    11.1.1.   Why Does It Matter? 54

11.2.   *SDLT Implications Of Transfers Involving A Mortgage* *56*

11.3.   *SDLT, Partnerships And Incorporation* *56*

11.4.   *Increased SDLT Risk For Companies – Indecision Costs Money!* *57*

11.5.   *Annual Tax On "Enveloped Dwellings" (ATED)* *57*

11.6.   *Foreign Ownership* *58*

11.7.   *How Limited is Your Liability?* *60*

12.   Close Companies **63**

12.1.   *What is a Close Company?* *63*

12.2.   *Special Rules for Close Companies* *63*

12.3.   *The Meaning of a "Distribution" From a Close Company* *64*

12.4.   *Loan To Participator* *64*

13.   The Directors' Tax Liabilities **68**

13.1.   *Tax on Non-Cash Benefits* *68*

13.2.   *Expenses* *68*
    13.2.1.   Travelling expenses 68
    13.2.2.   Cars 69
    13.2.3.   Using Your Own Car for Business 69

13.2.4.   Using Cars for Sole Traders and Partnerships 69
13.2.5.   Three Important Differences to Remember 69

13.3.   Other Expenses 70

13.4.   Shares as Rewards.. 70

13.5.   FOUR Tax Free Benefits... 72

14.   Companies and Tax Investigations 74

14.1.   "Aspect" Enquiries... 74

14.2.   "Compliance" Enquiries 74

14.3.   Full Enquiry.. 75

14.4.   "Grossing up"... 75

14.5.   Company Investigation Settlements 77

14.6.   Watch Out for the Contractual Disclosure Facility (CDF) and COP 9 79

14.7.   Four Golden Rules of Tax Investigations.. 79

15.   Getting Your Exit Strategy Right 80

15.1.   Everybody Has an Exit Strategy.. 80

15.2.   The THREE Most Common Exit Strategies 80

15.3.   Selling the Business.. 80
15.3.1.   Benefits of Buying the Shares in the Company............................. 80
15.3.2.   Drawbacks of Buying the Shares in the Company 81
15.3.3.   Benefits of Selling the Shares in the Company............................. 81
15.3.4.   Benefits of Selling the Company's Assets and then Liquidating 82

15.4.   Selling the Company's Shares 82
15.4.1.   "Earn-outs".. 82
15.4.2.   "Employment-Related Shares or Securities"................................ 84
15.4.3.   Payments Under Warranties and Indemnities 84
15.4.4.   "Compensation for Loss of Office"... 84
15.4.5.   Pre-Sale Tax Planning 84
15.4.6.   Company Purchase of Own Shares 84
15.4.7.   Timing 85
15.4.8.   Gifts to Spouse... 85
15.4.9.   Substantial Shareholding Exemption... 86
15.4.10.   Post-Sale Tax Planning 86
15.4.11.   Tax Shelters 86
15.4.12.   Losses 86

15.5.   Sales of Assets and Liquidation of Company.. 87

15.6.   How to Liquidate a Company 87
15.6.1.   A Formal Liquidation.. 87
15.6.2.   An Informal Liquidation 87
15.6.3.   Phoenix Arrangements 88

15.7.   Dying in Harness 89

16.   Inheritance Tax and Companies 90

16.1.   IHT – the Basics 90

16.2.   Nil Rate Band (NRB).. 90

16.3.   Residence Nil Rate Band (RNRB) 90

16.4.   PETs 92

16.5.	Gift with Reservation of Benefit	93
16.6.	Spouse Exemption	93
16.7.	Business Property Relief	94
16.8.	Close Companies and IHT	94

17. Finding an Accountant **97**

17.1.	Accountants Qualifications	97
17.2.	General Advisor or Tax Specialist?	98
17.3.	How to Choose Your Adviser	98
17.3.1.	Will I Need a Tax Adviser or an Accountant?	98
17.3.2.	What Qualifications?	98
17.3.3.	How Much Experience do they Have?	99
17.3.4.	How Much Will It Cost?	99
17.3.5.	Professional Bodies	99
17.3.6.	What About Indemnity Cover?	99
17.3.7.	How do I Contact My Tax Adviser / Accountant?	100
17.3.8.	Keep up to Date with Tax Legislation Changes	100
17.3.9.	What if I Have an Emergency?	101
17.3.10.	Does the Adviser Sell 'Off the Shelf' Packages?	101

18. The Importance of Tax Planning **102**

18.1.	Knowing When to Consider Planning	102
18.1.1.	Buying	102
18.1.2.	Repairs and Refurbishment	103
18.1.3.	Selling	103
18.1.4.	Life changes	104
18.1.5.	Politics	104
18.1.6.	End and Start of Tax Year	104
18.2.	The Real Benefits of Tax Planning	105
18.2.1.	Paying Less Tax	105
18.2.2.	Clear 'Entrance' and 'Exit' Strategies	105
18.2.3.	Staying Focused	105
18.2.4.	Improving Cash Flow	105
18.2.5.	Avoiding Common Tax Traps	106
18.3.	The Golden Tax Rules	106
18.3.1.	Education…Education…Education	106
18.3.2.	Prevention is Better Than Cure	106

19. International and Offshore Companies by Daniel Feingold **110**

19.1.	About Daniel Feingold	110
19.2.	Watch Out for the Single Solution Approach	110
19.3.	Using an Offshore Company	111
19.4.	The SEVEN pitfalls of using an Offshore Company	111
19.5.	Using Local Companies	115
19.6.	Using a Double Tax Treaty to Your Advantage	116
19.7.	CM&C and Local Companies	116
19.8.	Using a UK Company to Buy Overseas Property	116
19.9.	Foreign Branch Tax Rules	117
19.10.	Understanding Foreign Tax Rates	117

19.11.   *Extracting Money from Your UK Company* *117*

19.12.   *Using Two Companies* *118*

19.13.   *Using a Nominee Company* *119*

19.14.   *EFURBS* *119*

19.15.   *A Final Word* *120*

20.   Appendix A – Template Documents **122**

About Lee Sharpe

Lee is a Chartered Tax Adviser and tax consultant with over twenty years' experience in helping individuals, families, businesses and advisers with their tax affairs.

Lee writes extensively on tax matters for taxpayers and their advisers, including through the Tax Insider publications, Bloomsbury Professional and the TaxationWeb website. He also lectures taxpayers, accountants and other financial advisers on tax issues.

While he has appeared on TV to comment on tax matters, it was only long enough to establish that he really has a face for radio, and to give fellow members of his local CIOT branch sufficient ammunition with which to embarrass him at committee meetings.

When he is not giving tax advice or writing about tax matters, he is busy looking after his two small children – not because he likes them, but because he wants to make sure that his office is not used exclusively for business purposes…

About This Guide

One of the most common questions tax advisers often get asked is "should I use a limited company or not?"

There is no simple answer to this question, and there is a great deal of myth and misunderstanding about limited companies.

The purpose of this guide is to set out the benefits and drawbacks of using a limited company as a vehicle for a property business, and to compare them with other possible business structures.

Over the last few years, there has been a rush to *incorporate* (i.e., to transfer their business into a limited company) by many small businesses, egged on by the tax breaks introduced by the Chancellor of the Exchequer in 2000 and in 2002. These tax breaks were withdrawn with effect from April 2006, and as a result, the decision whether to incorporate or not has become more difficult.

Most notably, the 2015 Summer Budget heralded a significant increase in the effective rates of dividend taxation, such that company dividends have lost some of their shine. But the Chancellor also announced tax relief restrictions for Buy-to-Let landlords operating as individuals (whether solely, in joint names or in partnership) that left companies largely unaffected. In some sectors, the race is very much back on. People will, however, need to keep an eye on the current Chancellor, who seems to be alive to the potential savings to be made by operating through a company.

Unless otherwise indicated, we shall be using 2018/19 rates and allowances. 2017/18 saw the first tangible divergence in Scottish Income Tax rates when compared to the rest of the UK: for non-savings income; 2018/19 will see a significant divergence when comparing Scotland with the rest of the UK, as the Scottish government has not just moved thresholds this time but has introduced entirely new bands, and rates.

Interestingly for tax geeks, the Scottish devolved taxing powers basically cannot affect savings income (including dividends) so that the Scottish Higher Rate threshold for bank interest, dividends and the like will be £46,350 in 2018/19, just like the rest of the UK – which potentially makes for some quirky calculations around the c£43,000 - c£46,000 income band for Scottish taxpayers, depending on the mix of incomes at that level.

There are also potential knock-on implications, such as eligibility for the new Marriage Allowance. However, it should be emphasised that in very many cases, Scottish taxpayers will end up with similar results to rest-of-UK taxpayers and, even where they do not, the differences are likely to be relatively modest. **This book will apply the 'standard' UK rates and thresholds throughout.**

The Scottish tax regime also includes "Land and Buildings Transaction Tax" (LBTT) instead of the Stamp Duty Land Tax (SDLT) with which most readers will be familiar. From 1 April 2018, "Land Transaction Tax" will be payable in Wales, instead of SDLT. While very similar, there are differences between the three regimes, and readers operating in Scotland or Wales should get specific advice on LBTT and LTT respectively; this guide follows the SDLT regime such as it applies in the rest of the UK

This guide assumes you have no previous knowledge or experience of limited companies. By the time you finish it, we hope you will have a much clearer idea of the way a company works, and whether it is the right vehicle for your business.

1. Choosing the Right Structure

Anyone wishing to run a business in the UK has a wide choice of ways to organise it. Each possible structure has its own advantages and disadvantages.

This chapter gives an overview of the three basic types of business structures that are commonly used.

1.1. Sole Trader

This is the simplest form of business.

A sole trader owns and runs his business directly – he is "self-employed". All the risks and rewards are his directly, and all the decisions about the business are his.

If things go well he owns all the profits he has made (after he has paid tax on them!).

If things go badly, he is liable for all the debts of the business. He has "unlimited liability" – if his business fails, his private property can be taken to pay off the debts of the business. In other words, even his wealth outside of his business is at risk.

1.2. Partnership

Where two or more people own and run a business together, they are known as a partnership.

Like a sole trader, all the risks and rewards belong to the partners – but the crucial point is that EACH partner is JOINTLY liable for ALL of the partnership's debts.

If things go wrong, any money owed by the business can be recovered from the partners – and if one of them has no money to pay, the other partners will have to pay his share of the debts as well. Like the sole trader, a partner's liability is "unlimited" – even non-business personal wealth is at risk.

1.3. Limited Company

A Limited Company is a "legal person". This means that it exists independently of its shareholders, and it can make contracts, and be sued for its debts.

Here, the word "Limited" means that the shareholders' liability is limited to the money they have invested in their shares. If things go wrong, the worst that can happen to the shareholders is that they will not get their money back - though as we shall see, this is not in fact always the case.

1.4. Types of Partnerships

There is really only one kind of sole trader, but there are different kinds of partnership.

The basic type of partnership is defined by the Partnership Act 1890, and involves "persons carrying on a business in common with a view of profit".

A partnership is not a separate legal person from its members, and for tax purposes it is "transparent". In other words, the partnership itself does not pay tax – each partner pays tax on his share of the profits.

In Scotland, a partnership is a legal person, but for tax purposes, it is treated in the same way as an English partnership, and is "transparent" like them.

In some cases, although two people may agree to share the income from a project, they are not strictly a partnership because they are not carrying on "a business in common".

In such a case, the activity is commonly referred to as a "joint venture".

HM Revenue and Customs (HMRC) will sometimes claim that this is the case where a jointly owned property is rented out, and this can have significant tax consequences, as we shall see later.

We have seen how the partners in a partnership are jointly liable for the business debts.

There are some varieties of partnership where this is not entirely the case and these are detailed in the following sections.

1.4.1.   A "Limited Partnership"

A "Limited Partnership" is one where one or more of the partners has his liability limited to the capital he contributes to the partnership when he joins – like a shareholder, the worst that can happen to him is that he loses the money he invested, unlike an ordinary partner who might lose everything.

There are special rules for such partnerships:

- At least one of the partners must be a "general partner" who has unlimited liability, as in an ordinary partnership, and is responsible for running the business.

- A limited partner is not allowed to withdraw any of his capital from the partnership until he leaves the firm.

- A limited partner is not allowed to take part in running the partnership's business, or to make contracts, etc., on behalf of the firm – if he does, he loses his limited liability and becomes an ordinary partner.

- There are restrictions on how much relief such partners can have for any losses made by the partnership, and they cannot get tax relief for the interest on any money they borrow to invest in the partnership.

Such partnerships are rather specialised entities, but they can have their uses.

In other words, a limited partner must be a "sleeping partner" – that is, a partner who does not get involved in running the partnership.

1.4.2.   A Limited Liability Partnership (known as an LLP)

This is a fairly new sort of business entity, which was made possible by the Limited Liability Partnership Act 2000.

Unlike a normal partnership, it is a separate legal person from its members, but for tax purposes it is "transparent" like an ordinary partnership.

As the name implies, the partners in an LLP have limited liability, like shareholders in a company.

LLPs have proved popular with large professional firms such as accountants and solicitors, but as a general rule they are not appropriate for the smaller property investor or trader, being rather cumbersome to administer.

The idea of LLPs was that they would combine the advantages of a company (limited liability) with those of a partnership (informality and flexibility).

Some would say, however, that they also combine the disadvantages!

Except for unusual situations like Case Study - 1, the most suitable form of partnership for the property investor is likely to be the traditional Partnership Act type, as described above.

2. Getting to Grips with Limited Companies

In this chapter we will start to understand the structure of Limited Companies.

2.1. The Different Types of Limited Company

There are several types of Limited Company:

A Private Limited Company is the type we shall be concentrating on in this guide. It is the basic type of limited company, used by hundreds of thousands of businesses.

A Public Limited Company ("plc.") is allowed to raise funds by selling shares to the public, but it is also subject to much stricter legal controls than a Private Limited Company.

A Listed Company is a plc. whose shares can be traded on the Stock Exchange.

There are some other types of company, such as a **company limited by guarantee** – this is normally used by charities, and because it is not allowed to distribute its profits to its shareholders, it is ideal for that purpose – and useless for a property investor!

> For the rest of this guide, when we use the word "company" we shall be referring to a **private limited company**.

2.2. The Basic Rules for a Company

The basic rules for a company are:

- It must have at least one shareholder. The shareholders own the company, and their ownership is evidenced by the number of **shares** they own. If, for example, a company has a total of 100 shares issued to its shareholders, someone who owns 51 of those shares owns 51% of the company.

  He also **"controls"** the company, because in normal circumstances he will have 51 out of 100 votes if decisions are to be made about the company's policies.

- It must have at least one director. Directors are responsible for running the company's business affairs. The shareholders own the company, but the directors run it on a day to day basis. In the case of the typical smaller property business company, the directors are often the shareholders as well.

- A company must prepare and file accounts each year with Companies House (the government agency that regulates UK companies). These must be filed within 9 months of the end of the period covered by the accounts.

- A company must also file various returns of other information with Companies House, notifying such things as the appointment of new directors, and so on.

- A Company must have a **Memorandum and Articles of Association.** These are formal documents which set out the basic structure of the company – the number of shares it can issue, the rules for transferring shares from one person to another, and the purposes for which the company has been formed.

  Although these "Mem & Arts" are available as standard format documents, it is important to be sure that they are appropriate for your particular company.

  If necessary, the "Mem & Arts" can be altered or updated, but there is a formal process for doing this.

- Decisions made by the directors or shareholders of a company should be recorded in the company's **Minutes** – which comprise a formal record of such things as appointing new directors, issuing shares, or paying dividends.

  There is an example of a company **minute** in section 6.4.1 of this guide.

If this sounds a daunting list of tasks, do not despair – there are a number of specialist companies that offer help with these tasks, and your accountant will be able to advise you on compliance with the routine requirements.

> It is important to realise, however, that a company is a more formal structure than a sole trader or a partnership, and that there are penalties for failing to comply with the rules.

The accounts of a company must be prepared according to certain rules and in a certain format. **You will need an accountant to prepare these for you.**

Companies over two out of the three following thresholds are also required to have their accounts "audited" – that is, checked for accuracy by an independent accountant. These thresholds were increased in 2016 to:

- a turnover of over £10.2 million,
- assets of more than £5.1 million,
- an average of over 50 employees

Even if your company falls below these limits and an audit is not required, you should include the cost of having company accounts prepared by an accountant when you look at the figures for your company.

All the above requirements for companies mean that you should budget for at least £1,000 in "compliance" costs for each year – to cover preparation of accounts, submission of the various statutory returns, and working out the tax payable by the company.

This is a rough minimum figure – but it will be the one we shall use in the case studies that compare companies with other business entities.

Once a company has filed its accounts, they become **public information.**

Anyone (including your employees or your competitors) can access Companies House' website and get a copy of the accounts, together with information on the shareholders and directors of the company.

For companies that are excused from being audited, only "abridged" (previously referred to as "abbreviated") accounts need be filed and made public – "abridged" accounts do not show as much detail as full accounts (for example there may not be a profit and loss account) but nevertheless, they give quite a lot of information about the company.

3.   Understanding Corporation Tax

In this chapter we will understand the meaning of Corporation Tax ("CT") and will look at how this tax affects companies.

3.1.   The Rates of Corporation Tax

With effect from 1 April 2015, practically all companies pay Corporation Tax ("CT") on their profits – including their capital gains – at the same rate. This has fallen from 20% to 19% for profits arising after March 2017 and the government has said it intends a further reduction to 17% for profits from April 2020.

3.2.   Key Dates for the Company

A company must decide on the date to which it will prepare its accounts – its **accounting reference date.**

A company normally has the same accounting reference date every year, so that its **period of account** is the year ending on the accounting reference date.

If a company wishes, it can change its accounting reference date, so that the period of account in which the date is changed is longer or shorter than one year – but it cannot be longer than 18 months.

For the purposes of corporation tax, companies are taxed on the profits they make in their **accounting period.**

This is normally the same as the company's period of account, so that if a company's accounting date is 31 December (the most popular date, along with 31 March) then its period of account will be the year ending on 31 December, and its accounting period for corporation tax purposes will also be the year ending 31 December.

In some circumstances, there may be a difference between the company's period of account and its accounting period. This is because the tax legislation includes rules for when a company's accounting period ends, and these mean that an accounting period for tax purposes may end on a different day to the company's accounting date.

For corporation tax purposes, a company's accounting period (for tax purposes) comes to an end at the earliest of several dates, including:

- 12 months after it started (whereas a company's accounts may cover up to 18 months)

- The date the company chooses as its accounting date (so for example, if the accounting period begins on 1 January, and the company decides to change its accounting date to 31 October, it will have a 10-month accounting period for that year)

- The date the company becomes liable to corporation tax (such as when it gets a source of income) – or when it stops being so liable

- The date the company begins trading

- The date the company stops trading

- The date the **winding up** of the company begins (that is, when the process of ending the company's existence starts)

In cases where the company's accounting period (for tax) is not the same as its period of account, the tax inspector will apportion the profits of the period of account to arrive at the profits of the accounting period – this most often happens when the company's period of account is longer than one year.

The apportionment is normally done on a time basis, but the inspector (or the company) can look at the dates of specific transactions if this gives a fairer result – for example, if a large part of a car-dealing company's profit for the overall period of account came from one transaction, such as the sale of a vintage Ferrari, this could be put into the tax accounting period when it occurred rather than being apportioned or "spread" across more than one period.

3.3. Benefiting from the Favourable Company Taxes

Rates of tax for companies may seem very favourable, compared to income tax at 40% for taxable income over roughly £46,000, (including the tax-free Personal Allowance), and 45% for taxable income over £150,000.

Case Study - 2   Favourable Company Taxes

Bill has a property portfolio of 10 buy to let properties.

After all expenses, the rentals from these properties produce a profit of £20,000 per year. Because the portfolio is held within a company, the company must pay CT of £3,800 (£20,000 at 19%).

If Bill owned the properties directly, the income tax he would pay would depend on how much other income he had for the year, but it would probably be between £4,000 (£20,000 at 20%) and £8,000 (£20,000 at 40%).

The above case study, however, misses out the most important point about companies as compared to sole traders or partnerships – once the company has paid its CT for the year, the remaining cash still belongs to the company, not (yet) its shareholders/directors, and there may be further tax costs in extracting it.

3.4. Extracting the Cash from the Company

There are essentially two ways of extracting cash from a company and both these methods are described in the following sections.

3.4.1. *Paying a Salary*

If the company pays a salary, it will usually have to operate PAYE on that salary, just like any other employer. It will also have to deduct National Insurance Contributions, and pay employers' National Insurance Contributions.

Case Study - 3   Extracting Money Using a Salary

If Bill has no other income for the year, and the company pays all of its £20,000 profits out to him as a salary, the tax works like this:

Company Profit (after deducting salary)	NIL
Employers' NIC on Salary	(1,404)
Salary net of employers' NIC	18,596
Employees' NIC	(1,220)
Income tax	(1,349)
Cash in hand after PAYE	16,027
Effective rate of tax on £20,000	19.87%

If Bill had owned the properties directly, then his tax bill would have been:

Income from property	20,000
Deduct personal allowance	(11,850)
Taxable income	8,150
Income tax at 20%	(1,630)
Cash in hand after tax	18,370
Effective rate of tax on £20,000	8.15%

Note there is no National Insurance to pay where owned directly, because letting property is not a trade. National insurance was payable on the salary from the company, however, as it is on all salaries.

3.4.2. Paying Dividends

The other way for Bill to extract the cash from his company is for the company to pay him a **dividend**.

A dividend is how a company distributes its profits to its shareholders. Unlike paying a salary, a company cannot deduct the dividends it pays from its profits chargeable to CT.

When shareholders receive a dividend, the rate of tax they pay depends on their other income for the tax year. The rules for the taxation of dividends have changed markedly from April 2016. We shall use these new rules from now on in this book. If those shareholders are not liable to tax at the higher rate (taxable income exceeding the tax-free Personal Allowance over £34,500 for 2018/19), then the rate of income tax on their dividend is 7.5%. In the tax years running up to 2015/16, the effective tax rate for dividends up to the higher rate threshold was nil; now there is a tax-free Dividend Allowance that covers up to the first £2,000 of dividend income (it was initially set at £5,000 but Mr. Hammond decided that was far too generous and would be reduced to £2,000 for dividends paid after 5 April 2018 – i.e., 2018/19):

Basic Rate Taxpayer already	
Dividend paid	10,000
Less: Dividend Allowance	(2,000)
Taxable amount of dividend	8,000
Income tax on dividend at 7.5%	600

Note: Prior to 2016/17, there would have been **no** tax to pay on a dividend received by a basic rate taxpayer. In 2018/19, the tax cost of a £10,000 dividend will rise to £600.

If the shareholder is liable to income tax at the Higher Rate, then the rate of tax on their dividend will be the "Dividend Income rate" of 32.5%, and they still get the Dividend Allowance, so it works like this:

Higher Rate Taxpayer already	
Dividend paid	10,000

Less: Dividend Allowance	(2,000)
Taxable amount of dividend	8,000
Income tax on dividend at 32.5%	2,600

Note: Prior to 2016/17, the old rules would have meant that a Higher Rate taxpayer would have paid only £1,250 on a taxable cash dividend of £5,000. (There was also no Dividend Allowance before 2016/17)..

Case Study - 4   Extracting Money Using a Dividend

Mr Mean hates paying tax. For years, he has taken dividends up to the higher rate threshold and paid no tax. Based on the old dividend rules, he could take around £38,000 in dividends in 2015/16 and pay no tax.

He therefore arranges for his company to pay him a dividend in 2018/19 of £46,000, thinking that he will have no income tax to pay because he will not be in the higher rate band. (Including the standard tax-free Personal Allowance of £11,850 for 2018/19, the Higher Rate Threshold for this tax year is £46,350) Unfortunately for Mr. Mean, the new dividend rules apply:

Mr Mean	
Dividend paid	46,000
Deduct Dividend Allowance	(2,000)
Deduct standard Personal Allowance	(11,850)
Taxable dividend income	32,150
Dividend taxable at 7.5%	2,411

Mr. Mean will be horrified to learn that he is liable for £2,411 tax on his £46,000 dividend in 2018/19. However, if the company were to pay him a salary of £46,000 out of its profits instead, the combination of income tax and National Insurance would cost a further £5,200, even after factoring in the savings in corporation tax of paying a salary instead of dividends.

It seems clear, then, that dividends rather than salary are the way to extract cash from a company – but there can be cases where a mixture of the two provides the best solution.

3.4.3. *Paying Dividends and a Salary*

Case Study - 5   Extracting Money Using Both Dividend and a Salary (1)

Bill's property company makes a profit of £20,000 per year (see case study 3).

Bill has no other income for the year, so he pays himself a salary which is just below the "threshold" for income tax and NIC. The rest of the profit is paid out as a dividend:

	Company	Cash for Bill
Profit	20,000	
Deduct salary	(8,400)	8,400
Profit after salary	11,600	
Deduct CT on profit (19%)	(2,204)	
Profit after tax (dividend)	9,396	
Tax on Dividend	(296)	9,100
Total cash for Bill		17,500
Effective rate of tax	12.5%	

Bill has paid £870 more tax compared to the position if he had owned these properties directly (see Case Study 3), and in addition he would have had to pay the additional costs of running a company, which we have provisionally set at £1,000.

In broad terms, a company is unlikely to save enough money for a basic rate taxpayer (unless he has significant borrowings on residential properties – see later)

Let us look at the position for a higher rate taxpayer:

Case Study - 6   Extracting Money Using Both Dividend and a Salary (2)

Ben has other (non-dividend) income which means he pays income tax at the 40% Higher Rate. He also has a property portfolio in a company which, like Bill's, yields £20,000 profit per year.

He uses the same strategy as Bill, paying himself a salary just below the "threshold":

	Company	Cash for Ben
Profit	20,000	
Deduct salary	(8,400)	8,400
Profit after salary	11,600	
Deduct CT on profit (19%)	(2,204)	
Profit after tax (dividend)	9,396	
Income tax on dividend	(2,403)	6,993
Total cash for Ben		15,393
Effective rate of tax	23.03%	

If Ben had owned the properties directly, he would have paid 40% tax on the £20,000 profit (£8,000) and made £12,000, so he has apparently saved £3,393.

Because he has used £8,400 of his tax-free personal allowance against *this* salary, however, he will pay £3,360 more tax on his other (non-property) income, so he is practically no better off, particularly after factoring in the nominal extra £1,000 cost of running the company. (We are also ignoring any potential impact on the new "Savings Allowance" for bank and building society interest, which would further complicate matters).

The position would be worse if Ben decided to pay himself all in dividends. If so, the calculation would be:

	Company	Cash for Ben
Profit	20,000	
Deduct CT on profit	(3,800)	
Profit after tax (dividend)	16,200	
Income tax on dividend	(4,615)	
Total cash for Ben		11,585
Effective rate of tax	42.08%	

Although we are no longer "borrowing" £3,360 of salary tax against Personal Allowance used elsewhere, (because Ben is not taking a salary in this example), his net income of £11,585 is still £415 worse than if he'd just owned the rental portfolio directly – and that is before we consider the additional cost of running a company.

So far, we have seen that there is little or no advantage in using a company compared to owning property directly (see also the Tables in Appendix B, which lists anticipated savings or costs for incorporating a property investment business, at various net income levels). In certain situations, however, it can still produce savings, as we shall soon see.

4. Building Up a Property Portfolio Using a Company

In this chapter, we will look at when it is beneficial to use a company to **grow** a property portfolio.

4.1. Using a Company to Grow Your Property Portfolio

A company comes into its own when the plan is to reinvest the rental profits in more property, rather than to draw them out for living expenses.

Jane has a well-paid job, and pays income tax at 40%.

She wants to build up a portfolio of rented properties, using the profits from the rentals to fund the acquisition of other properties.

She begins with a portfolio of 10 buy to let properties in 2018, like Bill's, but instead of taking the profits out of the company, she leaves them there to fund the deposits on new properties.

In the first year, the position will be:

	Company	Direct ownership
Profits	20,000	20,000
Costs specific to company	(1,000)	NIL
Profit after costs	19,000	20,000
Tax payable	(3,610)	(8,000)
Cash for reinvestment	15,390	12,000

If the pattern is repeated in the following years, it is clear that she will be able to spend more money (within the company) on investing in new properties than she would if she were paying income tax on the rents. This relative saving will result in a "virtuous cycle", whereby each year will result in increasing better results, thanks to the lower Corporate Tax rate – which will improve even further, once the 17% rate starts in 2020/21.

In (say) 2025, Jane's company sells some of its properties. The disposals are subject to Corporation Tax on capital gains:

	Company	Direct ownership
Proceeds	500,000	500,000

Cost of properties	(200,000)	(200,000)
Capital Gain	300,000	300,000
Tax payable (17% / 28%)	(51,000)	(84,000)
Cash for reinvestment	449,000	416,000

The company benefits from a significantly lower tax rate than Jane would pay on residential property. The rate of Corporation Tax is set to fall to 17% in 2021/22. The net result is that the company pays not much more than half the tax that Jane would, if she owned the properties personally.

Note: Jane would normally have to pay more tax to access those funds in the company – the so-called "double tax charge", where the company pays tax on profits or gains, and then the shareholder/director pays tax to get the funds out of the company for personal use. These examples serve to illustrate how companies have the advantage if they are able to retain their profits to boost growth.

However, there is a new development that will, for many residential landlords, tip the balance strongly in favour of incorporation, whether they keep the profits in the company or not. That is the impending disallowance of finance costs in relation to the letting of residential property, which we shall look at next.

5. Disallowance of Mortgage Interest on Residential Properties

This measure was announced in the 2015 Summer Budget, and has been outraging residential property landlords ever since.

Generally, costs are fully deductible so long as they relate to the business – they are incurred "wholly and exclusively" for the property business (or are apportioned if appropriate, such as where only some of the expense is applied for business purposes). But since April 2017, (the 2017/18 tax year), interest relief has started to be disallowed for tax purposes only.

The key points are:
- The regime applies to all taxpayers that pay **income tax** – individuals, partners, trusts but **not** companies (which pay only 19% corporation tax anyway)
- It applies to any kind of financing deal, not just a simple 'mortgage'
- It applies to any kind of financial cost, not just 'interest'
- It applies to residential properties; commercial properties are ignored.
- Where there are borrowings against both commercial and residential properties, the amount to be disallowed should be apportioned on a "just and reasonable basis".
- While property **developers** are not generally caught, someone financing the development of a property with the intention of ultimately letting it out, rather than for onward sale, **is** subject to the new rules.
- Each tax year from 2017/18 through to 2020/21, a further 25% of the landlord's finance costs will be disallowed, to be replaced by a maximum 20% tax "credit", (strictly, a reduction in her tax bill), regardless of the landlord's actual marginal tax rate.

Case Study - 7   Disallowance of Mortgage Interest On Properties

Andrea has a portfolio of almost 20 residential properties that, up 'til now, have been generating around £60,000 of rental profits – after £80,000 of annual mortgage interest. She is therefore already a 40% taxpayer, despite having no other income. Assuming everything else stays broadly consistent for the next 4 years as well (so using 2016/17 rates throughout for ease of comparison to the year just before the new regime starts):

In 2016/17, Andrea will have paid tax on £60,000 – the last year before the new rules started to 'bite'.

In 2017/18, she will have paid tax on profits of £60,000 + (25% x £80,000 in annual interest) = £80,000. The extra £20,000 will get taxed at 40%, costing £8,000 in tax. She does, however, get a tax credit of 20% x £20,000 = £4,000, so in 2017/18 she owes a further net amount of **£4,000** in tax.

In 2018/19, she will pay tax on profits of £60,000 + (50% x £80,000 in annual interest) = £100,000. The extra £40,000 will get taxed at 40%, costing £16,000 in tax. She will get a tax credit of 20% x £40,000 = £8,000, so by 2018/19 she will owe a further **£8,000** in tax (against 2016/17).

In 2019/20, she will pay tax on profits of £60,000 + (75% x £80,000) = £120,000. The extra £60,000 will get taxed at 40%, but she will also forfeit most of her tax-free Personal Allowance because, for tax purposes only, she has exceeded £100,000 income. This will end up costing £28,000 in tax. She will get a tax credit of 20% x £60,000 = £12,000, so in 2019/20 she will owe a further **£16,000** in tax (against 2016/17). **Note the significant increase in tax liability this year, as the tax adjustment costs her most of her Personal Allowance.**

In 2020/21, she will pay tax on profits of £60,000 + (100% x £80,000) = £140,000. The extra £80,000 will get taxed at 40%, but she will also forfeit the last of her tax-free Personal Allowance because, for tax purposes only, she has exceeded £100,000 income. This will end up costing £36,400 in tax. She will get a tax credit of 20% x £80,000 = £16,000, so in 2020/21 she will owe a further **£20,400** in tax (against 2016/17).

So, by the time these new measures are fully implemented, Andrea's tax bill will have risen by £20,400 – roughly 150% – even though her real profits have not moved. Given that companies are not "caught" by this new regime, it will come as no surprise that they offer a relatively safe haven to landlords who might otherwise face the very real prospect of catastrophic business failure.

The above model used 2016/17 rates, etc., throughout to explain the concept. A more accurate summary now using later rates and allowances where known, comparing this with the alternative scenario of taking that same business model through a company, with a modest salary of around £8,000 and the balance of available profits as dividends, is set out below:

Tax Year:	2016/17 £	2017/18 £	2018/19 £	2019/20 £	2020/21 £
Net Rent after Mortgage	60,000	60,000	60,000	60,000	60,000
Add-back Rental Finance	0	20,000	40,000	60,000	80,000
Total	60,000	80,000	100,000	120,000	140,000
Net income personally	46,800	43,300	39,640	31,640	27,500
Net if taken through Co.	44,898	45,792	46,509	46,509	48,166
Saving if Co. instead	(1,902)	2,492	6,869	14,869	20,666

Note:

The model uses future rates and allowances where known, such as where the corporation tax rate falls in April 2020.

Using this model, Andrea's net-of-tax income will have almost halved by 2020/21 if she continues running the business on her own account. If she is able to transfer her business into a company, however, it will be protected from the worst effects of the new regime. For further information, please see Chapter 8 (Offsetting interest charges before 6th April 2017 and Chapter 9 (Offsetting interest charges after 6th April 2017) of the book called "How to Avoid Landlord Taxes".

6. Everything You Need to Know About Dividend Payments

We have been talking about companies paying dividends, and it is important to understand the rules that apply to such payments.

In this chapter we will examine these rules more closely.

6.1. Working with "Distributable Profits"

A company can pay a dividend only out of its "distributable profits".

"Distributable profits" are a company's profits after paying its expenses and its corporation tax.

If it does not pay any dividends for a particular year, then those "distributable profits" will remain in the company's balance sheet, and can be used to pay a dividend next year:

Case Study - 8   Distributing the Profits

A new company is set up, and in its first two years, it makes a profit of £40,000 per year after all expenses. Its distributable profits are therefore:

Profit for year 1	40,000
CT due on profit	(7,600)
Distributable profits	32,400
Profit for year 2	40,000
CT due on profit	(7,600)
Distributable profits	64,800

In the third year, the company has a bad year, and makes a loss of £10,000 after all expenses. Its distributable profits are now:

Distributable profits at start of year	64,800
Deduct loss for year	(10,000)
Repayment of corporation tax on loss	1,900
Distributable profits at end of year	56,700

Things go better in the fourth year, with a profit of £15,000, and the company decides to pay a dividend of £10,000:

Distributable profits at start of year	56,700
Add profit for year	15,000
Deduct CT due on profit	(2,850)
Distributable profits	68,850
Dividend paid	(10,000)
Distributable profits at end of year	58,850

6.2. Who Gets the Dividends?

Dividends are paid to the company's shareholders according to how many shares they own – so in a simple case where all the shares are of the same "class", each shareholder gets a dividend proportionate to his shareholding.

Case Study - 9   Apportioning the Dividends

The shares in a company are owned as follows:

Mary Jones (wife)	40 £1	Ordinary Shares
Joe Jones (husband)	40 £1	Ordinary Shares
Sue Jones (adult daughter)	20 £1	Ordinary Shares
Total	100 £1	Ordinary Shares

If the company pays a dividend of £10,000, that is equivalent to £100 per share, so the three shareholders will each receive:

Mary	£4,000
Joe	£4,000
Sue	£2,000
Total	£10,000

6.3. The Two Types of Dividend

It is important that the formalities are properly observed when a company pays dividends. There are two basic types of dividend:

6.3.1.   *A "Final" Dividend.*

This is a dividend paid out of the company's distributable profits after its accounting period ends.

The shareholders approve the company's accounts for the year, and also approve the payment of a "final" dividend, which is then said to have been "declared".

Although the final dividend may not in fact be paid until some time later, it is treated as payable for income tax purposes on the day it is "declared" (typically, when the accounts are approved), unless the declaration specifies a different date for the payment.

6.3.2.   *An "Interim" Dividend.*

This is a dividend paid by a company during the year. It is approved by the directors of the company, who must be satisfied there are enough "distributable reserves" to pay the dividend. For income tax purposes, an interim dividend is treated as paid on the date it is actually paid.

It is <u>essential</u> that the directors are satisfied there are sufficient distributable profits before they approve the payment of an interim dividend, and this means having accurate and up to date records of the company's income and expenses.

We shall see below what can happen if the directors pay a dividend without taking this precaution.

6.4.   Getting the Paperwork Right

It is also essential to produce the correct paperwork for a dividend. This means having:
- A minute of the meeting at which it was decided to pay the dividend

- A "dividend confirmation" for each shareholder

6.4.1.   *Sample – Meeting Minute*

Here is a sample wording for the minute of a resolution to pay an interim dividend:

Property Company Limited
Company Registration No. 12345678

1, Any Road
Anywhere
PO1 1PO

Minutes of a Meeting of the Board of Directors

Date of the meeting held at the Registered Office of the Company: **02/04/18**

Present:

Mr Joseph Jones (Director)
Mrs Susan Jones (Director)

DIVIDENDS

It was resolved that the company pay an interim dividend in respect of the period ending **31/12/18** to holders registered as at **02/04/18** as follows:

Share class	Dividend rate	Date to be paid
Ordinary of £1	**£100 per share**	**02/04/18**

ANY OTHER BUSINESS:

There being no further business the meeting was closed.

J Jones
………………………………………....
Signed on Behalf of the Board

Name: J Jones   Date: 02/04/18   Position: Director

Notice that the amount of the dividend is expressed as so much *per share*.

6.4.2. *Sample – Dividend Confirmation*

Here is an example of a dividend confirmation. One of these must be given to each shareholder when the dividend is paid:

Property Company Limited

Company Registration No. 12345678

1, Any Road
Anytown
PO1 1PO

Dividend Confirmation

Interim dividend for the period ending 31st December 2018 to shareholders registered on 2nd April 2018

Payment Date
02/04/18

Shareholder Details
Mrs Mary Jones
1, Any Road
Anytown
PO1 1PO

Shareholding	Dividend rate	Dividend Payment
40 Ordinary shares of £1	**£100 per share**	**£4,000**

This confirmation should be kept as part of your financial records.

Susan Jones
....
(director)

Date:

It may seem a nuisance putting this paperwork in place, but too many companies get themselves into trouble by not doing this properly.

6.5. Two Pitfalls to Avoid when Making Dividend Payments

Two of the commonest problems with company dividends are:

6.5.1. *Illegal Dividends.*

If the company pays a dividend that cannot be covered by its distributable profits, the shareholders will have to repay the dividend to the company, and they and the company may be taxed on the basis that instead of paying them a dividend, the company made a loan to them.

The company would also have to pay tax at 32.5% on the amount of the "loan", and this tax will be repaid to the company only when the shareholders have repaid the dividend. (**Note:** the tax rate increased from 25% to 32.5% for amounts advanced on or after 6 April 2016).

6.5.2. *Timing of Dividends*

Too often, a company's shareholders simply draw the cash they need from the company, and then declare a dividend at the end of the year equivalent to the cash they have taken from the company.

If this practice is discovered by HMRC, such as during an investigation of the company, the onus will be on the shareholders to prove that the cash they took out during the year was a loan from the company, which was repaid by the dividends declared after the end of the year, and not a disguised salary (on which, of course, PAYE and NIC will be due).

6.6. Using Dividend Waivers – An Effective Tax Planning Tool

It is possible for a shareholder to waive his right to a dividend.

This might be done because he has had enough income for the year, and does not want to pay tax on the dividend when he does not need the money.

Provided the following issues are carefully considered, a dividend waiver can be an effective tax planning tool.

Caution

Take care – dividend waivers are likely to be closely looked at by HMRC to see if they have been done properly, and there may be extra tax to pay if they are not.

A dividend cannot be waived once it has become payable, so interim dividends must be waived before they are paid, but final dividends must be waived before they are declared.

The waiver will take the form of a written document in which the shareholder gives up his right to the dividend. This should be in the form of a Deed, and **you may want to take advice to ensure that the paperwork is legally effective**.

The minutes of the meeting at which the dividend is paid (interim) or declared (final) should include a reference to the fact that the directors were shown a waiver of the dividend due to Mr X, and make it clear this was done before the dividend was declared or paid.

6.7. Watch out for the "Settlements" Legislation

It is essential that the waiver cannot be attacked under the "settlements" legislation. It is easiest to explain this with an example.

Case Study - 10   "Settlements" Legislation

Before the meeting at which the dividend in Case Study - 9 is paid, Joe (who pays tax at 40%) decides he does not want a dividend from the company, because he and Mary (who only pays tax at the basic rate) have enough other income for the year and Joe would prefer not to pay income tax on a dividend he does not need. He has a Dividend Waiver drafted by his solicitor and "executes" it (this is lawyer-speak for signing it in front of a witness) then gives it to his daughter Sue, the company secretary.

The interim dividend of £100 per share is therefore paid to Mary and Sue, but not to Joe:

	Company	Mary	Joe	Sue
Distributable profits	10,000			
Dividends Paid	(6,000)	4,000	Waived	2,000
Distributable profits	4,000			

This should be acceptable to HMRC, but supposing the company decided to pay a dividend of £150 per share:

	Company	Mary	Joe	Sue
Distributable profits	10,000			
Dividends Paid	(9,000)	6,000	Waived	3,000
Distributable profits	1,000			

HMRC will argue that of that £9,000 dividend, £3,000 should be taxed on Joe!

This may seem illogical at first, but consider what would have happened if Joe had not waived his right to a dividend, and a payment of £150 per share had been made:

	Company	Mary	Joe	Sue
Distributable profits	10,000			
Dividends Paid	(15,000)	6,000	6,000	3,000
Distributable profits	**Minus 5,000, so Illegal dividend if no waiver**			

In other words, the only reason why the company was able to pay Mary £6,000 and Sue £3,000, instead of £4,000 and £2,000 respectively, **was because Joe had waived his right to his dividends.**

HMRC will say that Joe has made a "settlement" of £3,000 of his income on Sue and Mary. This is a highly technical area of the law, and there are arguments against HMRC's point of view, but what is certain is that using a waiver in this way is likely to lead to time-consuming and expensive enquiries from HMRC.

7. The Property Development Company

Much of what we have covered so far has been from the perspective of a property investor, although the basics of company law and dividends apply pretty much universally. In this chapter, will now consider some aspects specific to the property developer.

7.1. The Property Developer

A **property developer** buys property (or sometimes bare land) with the intention of improving the property (or building a new property) and selling it on in the short term, at a profit. By contrast, a property investor holds on to his or her property more for the long term, generally with an expectation of capital growth but without a short term profit motive

> The important distinction for tax purposes is that a property developer is **trading**.

The property developer will pay income tax on the profits he makes from selling the properties, whereas the property investor will pay capital gains tax if and when he sells one of his investment properties.

An individual who is trading in property will also be liable to pay National Insurance Contributions (NICs) on his profits, unless he is over the state pension age (depending on a person's exact date of birth – the qualifying age is being increased for women, to equal that of men, and then increased for both sexes to 67).

7.2. Companies and Property Developers

This gives us a rather different picture when we compare trading as an individual property developer with doing the same thing through a company.

Case Study - 11	Using a Company for Your Property Development Activities

Dave trades as a property developer through a limited company. He has other income from investments, so he pays income tax at 40%. His company makes a profit of £100,000 for the year. If he draws out all the profits from the company as dividends, plus a salary just below the "threshold" (see Case Study 5), his tax position will be:

	Company	Cash for Dave	If no company	Saving
Profit	100,000		100,000	
Salary	(8,400)	8,400		

	Company	Cash for Dave	If no company	Cost
Company running costs	(1,000)			
Profit	90,600			
CT due (at 19%)	(17,214)			
Distributable profit (dividend)	73,386	73,386		
Income tax		(23,200)	(40,000)	
NIC			(4,639)	
Cash for Dave		58,586	55,361	3,225

Of course, as in Case Study 6, he will pay an extra £3,360 tax on his investment income because he has used £8,400 of his personal allowance against his salary, so he has basically "broken even".

If Dave had a large salary from another job, so that he could not take advantage of the "below the threshold" salary from his company, the position would be:

	Company	Cash for Dave	If no company	Cost
Profit	100,000		100,000	
Company running costs	(1,000)			
Profit	99,000			
CT due (at 19%)	(18,810)			
Distributable profit (dividend)	80,190	80,190		
Income tax		(25,411)	(40,000)	
NIC			(1,987)*	
Cash for Dave		54,779	58,013	(3,234)

* Because Dave has a substantial salary from another job, his Class 4 self-employed contributions will be restricted to those at the 2% rate. He will still be liable for the weekly Class 2 contribution, however (at least for 2018/19).

Note: In practice, Dave would pay more income tax than shown, because on taxable income between £100,000 and £123,700, his personal allowance of £11,850 would be withdrawn at a rate of £1 for every £2 of income. As this applies whether incorporated or not, it has been ignored for simplicity.

Once again, it is clear that there may be little tax advantage in using a company if you are going to want to extract all the profits for your personal use. It may depend on how much NIC you may save by incorporating the business, compared to how much extra tax you may have to pay – first on company profits, and then on dividends to extract the net funds.

Incorporation *can* offer some savings, where it is possible to utilise the comparatively low tax rate of 7.5% that applies where dividends are taxed below the Higher Rate Threshold, which is £46,350 (except in Scotland, as already noted). However, it must be noted that the profit ranges at which substantive savings can be made, can be quite narrow:

Case Study - 12	Using a Company for Your Property Development Activities – No Other Income

Diane trades as a property developer and is contemplating the transfer of her business into a limited company. If she draws out all the profits from the company as dividends, plus a salary just below the "threshold" (see Case Study 5), her tax position will be:

	Company	Cash for Diane	If no company	Saving
Profit	55,000		55,000	
Salary	(8,400)	8,400		
Company running costs	(1,000)			
Profit	45,600			
CT due (at 19%)	(8,664)			
Distributable profit (dividend)	36,936	36,936		
Income tax		(2,361)	(10,360)	

NIC			(3,740)	
Cash for Diane		42,975	40,900	2,075

This is quite a substantial tax saving, but note that running a comparison at £45,000 in net profits would net only a £550 saving, and £35,000 in profits would save less than £200 on incorporation. (Simpler models may indicate greater savings, but they will ignore the extra costs of running a company, set here at £1,000).

Larger savings can be made where trading profits exceed £100,000 but as profits rise much beyond £120,000, the net saving quickly turns to a net loss. See the Tables in Appendix B for further details of the savings / costs of incorporation, for various profit levels.

If your strategy is to leave the profits in the company and use them to finance further development, however, having a property development company will offer similar cumulative tax benefits as it does to a property investor – see section 4.1

If you are already trading as a property developer, as a sole trader or a partnership, and you feel it would be beneficial to transfer the business into a company so as to take advantage of the lower rates of tax on your profits, there is an important relief from tax you can take advantage of – **incorporation relief**. This is dealt with later in this guide (see Chapter 8).

7.3.   The Construction Industry Scheme ("CIS")

An important note on the Construction Industry Scheme ("CIS")

The CIS requires property developers to deduct tax from certain payments to tradesmen, and in other cases to record amounts paid and make regular returns to HMRC of those amounts. The details of this scheme are beyond the scope of this guide, but a number of smaller property development businesses are not aware that they come within this scheme, and as a result may face penalties for failure to operate the scheme. There is no minimum level below which the scheme does not apply to a property developer.

The CIS does not normally apply to buy to let **investors** unless they spend over £1million on construction work each year, (although HMRC may try to argue that CIS applies even to property investors for the duration of a significant construction project), but it does apply to ALL property **developers**.

Further details of the CIS can be found in **"Tax Secrets for Property Developers and Renovators"**, which is available through www.property-tax-portal.co.uk.

8.   Incorporation Relief

In this chapter we will look at a CGT relief that is potentially available when business assets are transferred into a company that you control.

This relief is known as Incorporation Relief.

8.1.   Transferring Assets into Your Company

If you transfer any asset you own to a company that you control, for tax purposes you will be treated as having disposed of it at its current market value, so you may well find yourself making a capital gain and paying CGT.

There are, however, two forms of tax relief that may help to solve this problem and these are detailed in the following sections.

8.1.1.   Holdover Relief for Gifts of Business Assets

This applies when a person carrying on a trade makes a gift of an asset used for that trade, or sells it at less than its market value.

Where an asset is gifted or sold at less than its market value, a claim can be made to "hold over" the gain on the **difference between the market value of the asset, and the amount (if any) actually paid for it.**

Case Study - 13   Holdover Relief

Rita owns five cottages, which she bought seven years ago with a legacy from her grandmother, and which she lets out to tourists as "furnished holiday accommodation". This is treated as a trade for CGT purposes (see **"Tax Secrets for Property Developers and Renovators"** for details of how a property can qualify as "furnished holiday accommodation").

The cottages each produce a rental profit of £10,000 per year.

Rita does not intend to sell these cottages – she regards them as her "pension fund" and would like to be able to leave them to her children when she dies.

At the moment, she has a highly paid job, and does not need all the income from these cottages, so her Tax Adviser suggests that she might benefit from transferring these cottages into a company.

She bought each cottage seven years ago for £50,000, and they are now worth £150,000 each, so she would make a capital gain of £100,000 on each cottage. As these are qualifying holiday cottages, she will be eligible for Entrepreneurs' Relief (see Chapter 9) and so pay CGT at only 10%. The potential CGT exposure is (£100,000 x 5 = £500,000 - £11,700 Annual Exemption = £488,300) @ 10% = £48,830.

Her Tax Adviser suggests she set up a company, and sell the cottages to it for £52,340 each, and make a claim to "hold-over" the rest of the gain.

He explains that the tax calculation will work like this:

"Sale" proceeds of 5 cottages	**261,700**
Less cost of cottages	**(250,000)**
Capital gain	**11,700**
Annual CGT exempt amount for 2018/19	**(11,700)**
Taxable gains for year	**NIL**
CGT	**NIL**

The balance of the capital gain – originally £500,000 but now reduced to £488,300 – has been held over, and will be chargeable when the company sells or otherwise disposes of the properties.

The company does not necessarily need to pay Rita £261,700 in cash. Instead it credits her with having lent this money to the company. Rita will be able to draw this loan out of the company as and when she needs the money, and without paying any income tax.

Meanwhile, the company is only paying 19% tax (in 2018) on the rents it receives, instead of the 40% income tax Rita was paying. On the combined rental profits of £50,000, this is a tax saving of a little over £10,000 per year.

There is one downside to this, however. For the purposes of Stamp Duty Land Tax, the properties are treated as transferred to the company at their market value, and so the company will have to pay SDLT on £750,000, which will cost it £25,000. The five properties are residential properties so the rate of SDLT is based on the average price per property (£150,000), subject to tiered rates (at a minimum of 3% for corporate acquisitions) of the whole sale proceeds (known as "**Multiple Dwellings Relief**").

Rita must decide if this up-front cost is worth paying.

Note that this strategy is specific to Rita's circumstances, and in particular to the fact that she intends to leave the holiday cottages to her children.

If she intended to sell them herself, she would probably do better to keep them in her personal ownership, because of the 10% rate of CGT she will pay on the gain, compared to 19% that the company would pay (although she *might* be able to find a buyer willing to acquire her company shares, whose sale may also qualify for Entrepreneurs' Relief, rather than the actual properties themselves).

8.1.2.   *Incorporation in Exchange for Shares*

There is another type of incorporation relief, which applies when a business is transferred to a company and instead of paying cash, the company issues shares in exchange for the assets.

It works like this:

Case Study - 14   Incorporation in Exchange for Shares

Bill has a business with a market value of £100,000. If he were to sell it for that sum, he would make a capital gain of (say) £70,000. He sets up a company, and transfers the business to the company. The company does not pay him anything for the business. Instead, it issues 1,000 £1 Ordinary shares to him.

From the company's point of view, it now owns a business worth £100,000, and the "cost" of that business from the company's point of view is £100,000 – so if it sold the business tomorrow, it would not make a capital gain.

From Bill's point of view, he now owns 1,000 shares worth £100 each (value of company = £100,000, divided by the 1,000 shares).

Because he qualifies for "Incorporation relief" on this transaction, he is not charged any capital gains tax, but the gain he would have been taxed on is deducted from the "cost" of his shares for CGT purposes, so the cost of his shares is deemed to be £30 each (£100,000 - £70,000 = £30,000, divided by the 1,000 shares). This is Bill's original CGT "base cost" for his business, pre-incorporation.

The fact that the company is treated as acquiring the business at its market value offers another planning opportunity:

Case Study - 15   Incorporation Followed by Sale of Business

John has a trading business with a market value of £2,000,000. He wants to sell it, and use the sale proceeds to buy a portfolio of investment properties, which he sees as his "retirement fund".

If he simply sold the business, he would make a capital gain of (say) £1,600,000, on which CGT of £160,000 would be due, assuming he qualifies for entrepreneurs' relief.

Instead, he transfers the business to a company in exchange for shares. The company issues 1,000 shares to him in exchange for the business. The position is therefore:

The company now owns the business, which for capital gains purposes "cost" it £2,000,000. John has 1,000 shares worth £2,000,000, but which for CGT

---

purposes "cost" him £400,000 (after deducting the held-over capital gain of £1,600,000).

The company now sells the business for £2,000,000. Because its cost to the company was £2,000,000, the company makes no gain at all and has no tax to pay. The company can spend the whole £2,000,000 on investment properties, and John should have a more comfortable retirement than if he had sold the business himself. John may still have to pay income tax on any funds he draws out of the business, but he can control exactly how much he takes, and how he is taxed – such as making best use of the (still) relatively low rates applicable to dividends.

8.2. Watch Out for Three Pitfalls

The previous case study looks almost too good to be true, and like most such things, there are a number of pitfalls that one needs to be wary of.

These pitfalls are:

8.2.1. "Preordained Series of Transactions"

There is a rule of law developed by the courts which allows HMRC to disregard a transaction if it is part of a series of transactions which were set up in advance, and the transaction in question was "inserted" simply for the purpose of avoiding tax.

In other words, HMRC might say that the reality was that John sold the business himself, and the transfer to the company was "inserted" purely for tax avoidance. For this reason, it would be most important that John had not started the process of selling the business before he transferred it to the company.

Anyone contemplating using the same strategy as John should take advice from a Tax Adviser on whether HMRC would be likely to attack it as "preordained".

8.2.2. Stamp Duty Land Tax

As we have already seen, SDLT is charged on the market value of a property when it is transferred to a company, so if a substantial part of the value of John's business was in any property it owned, there would be an SDLT cost to factor into the equation.

8.2.3. What is a "Business"?

The legislation uses the word "business", but HMRC interpret the meaning of this word quite narrowly. In particular, they take the view that a property investment business may not automatically qualify as a "business" for the purposes of incorporation relief.

There have been cases where property investment businesses have been transferred to companies and managed to get incorporation relief. Where the business involves a number of properties and involves a lot of management work, it is possible that HMRC would not dispute the relief, but each case needs to be looked at on its merits, and there can be no guarantees that there will not be a challenge from HMRC (although it may be possible to get "clearance" from HMRC beforehand).

In some cases, however, it may be worthwhile taking the risk.

8.3. Incorporating an Existing Property Investment Portfolio

Case Study - 16	Incorporating an Investment Portfolio

Jill has a business of exactly the same value as John's in Case Study - 15, but it consists of several commercial properties. She wants to sell these, and invest the money in buying a hotel.

She has been to a leading Tax Counsel, who has advised her that there is a good chance that her business would qualify for incorporation relief. He stresses that there is still a risk that it could be challenged by HMRC, however.

If Jill simply sells her properties, she will make a gain of £1,600,000, just like John. Her investment properties do not qualify for Entrepreneurs' Relief, however, so her CGT bill would be around £318,000 (using the new, lower, CGT rates applicable from April 2016 for **non**-residential property gains). If she transfers the business to a company and her incorporation relief is NOT denied by HMRC, the only cost will be the SDLT of £89,500 on the transfer of the properties to the company. Note that as these are not residential properties, the SDLT rate is determined by the total market value (and at different rates to those applicable to residential properties).

If the incorporation relief is denied, she will pay CGT of £318,000, but the company will still make no capital gain. It will, however, have paid the £89,500 SDLT.

Jill must decide if the *possible* saving of £318,000 CGT is worth the extra cost of £89,500 SDLT. The risk can be reduced by applying for "non-statutory clearance" from HMRC.

9. Entrepreneurs' Relief ("ER") from CGT

This was introduced for gains made after 5 April 2008, and replaced the old "Taper Relief".

It is a cumulative lifetime allowance of £10,000,000, applicable to gains on disposals of qualifying business assets. Instead of being charged at the more common 20%, the first £10 million of such gains are charged to tax at 10%.

"Business Assets" are strictly defined:

- A disposal of a sole trading business, or an interest in a partnership, provided it is a trading business and not an investment business

- A disposal of "part of a business" – this has to be an identifiable part of the business, not just an asset used in the business, so for example, a farmer could not claim ER on the sale of a few of his fields, but he could if he sold his pasture, milking parlour, and milk quota, while keeping his arable land – that would be a sale of a "part" of his business (the dairying part).

- An associated sale of assets used in the business, alongside the disposal of a substantive interest in, or (at least partly) retiring from, or ceasing the business.

- A sale of shares in a trading company, provided the shareholder was an employee or a director of the company, AND had held at least 5% of the voting shares for at least one year before the sale.

There is now a separate form of relief available for long-term investors in eligible trading companies. This will allow 'external' investors, who are not otherwise involved in the business, to benefit from the 10% rate, provided they subscribe for new shares and hold on to them for at least 3 years from 6 April 2016.

The detailed rules for Entrepreneurs' Relief and the similar Investors' Relief are complicated, and you should consult a Tax Adviser if you think you might qualify for either, on a sale/disposal that you are contemplating.

10. Reinvestment Relief

In this chapter we will look at "Reinvestment Relief". Numerous questions are asked about this relief and we will try to get to grips with the most common scenarios when this relief may be considered.

10.1. Property Investors and Reinvestment Relief

Property investors often ask if they can defer paying CGT on gains they have made by reinvesting the money in another property.

Unfortunately, this is generally not possible.

There are only two exceptions:

10.1.1. Business Assets

A company (or an individual or partnership) which is carrying on a trade can claim "rollover relief" from tax on its capital gains if it sells an asset it has used for its trade and spends **all the sale proceeds** on buying another asset to use in its trade.

The new asset must be purchased within the period that begins one year before the old asset is sold, and ends three years after that sale.

There are several categories of asset that qualify for this relief, and among them are land and buildings that are occupied and used for the purposes of the trade being carried on.

This type of rollover relief is **unlikely** to be of much use to the property business. It will not apply to the buy to let investor, because he is not carrying on a trade, and it will not apply to the buildings sold by a property developer, because these buildings are his trading stock and he makes a profit chargeable to income tax when he sells them, not a capital gain. But it could apply to his business premises, or other assets used in the trade.

10.1.2. Furnished Holiday Lettings

These are a special category of buy to let property – see Case Study - 13 – and rollover relief is available if one of these specially eligible properties is sold and the proceeds used to buy another eligible property.

Case Study - 17   Furnished Holiday Lettings and Reinvestment Relief

---

Chris owns a cottage which he lets according to the rules for "furnished holiday accommodation" (see "**Tax Secrets for Property Developers & Renovators**" for details of these rules). The cottage cost him £50,000 six years ago, and he sells it for £200,000.

The gain of £150,000 will qualify for ER because this type of letting is deemed to be a trade for some tax purposes, so he has a taxable gain of £150,000, on which he would pay £15,000 at the 10% tax rate (assuming his CGT Annual Exemption has already been used).

Chris spends £220,000 on another holiday cottage one year after the sale of the old one. He has effectively used the entire amount of the sale proceeds from the old cottage to buy the new one, so all of the capital gain on the old cottage is "rolled over" into the new one. When Chris comes to sell the new cottage, its cost for the purposes of CGT will be reduced by the amount of the gain that has been rolled over into it:

Amount spent on new cottage	220,000
Deduct capital gain rolled over from old cottage	(150,000)
Cost of new cottage for CGT purposes	70,000

.

There is some relief even if you do not reinvest all of the sale proceeds. Suppose that the new cottage cost Chris only £180,000. This is less than the sale proceeds of the old cottage, so the computation goes like this:

First, find the amount of the sale proceeds not reinvested. Here, this is £20,000 (£200,000 - £180,000). This is less than the capital gain of £150,000 on the old cottage, so the amount of the gain that has not been reinvested is £20,000.

Chris will be taxed on a gain of £20,000, (again potentially subject to Entrepreneurs' Relief) and the cost for CGT purposes of the new cottage will be:

Amount spent on new cottage	180,000
Deduct capital gain rolled over from old cottage	(130,000)
Cost of new cottage for CGT purposes	50,000

There is one other point to bear in mind about furnished holiday accommodation.

Because it would be possible for a person to roll a gain on an old holiday cottage over into a new one, and then move into it as his main residence and so "exempt" it from CGT, the relief is only given provisionally and if, when the new property is sold, it qualifies for relief from CGT as a main residence, the gain previously held over is brought back into charge.

There is another way to defer a capital gain by reinvesting into specially qualifying companies. This is by using the **Enterprise Investment Scheme ("EIS")** for individuals. This is a scheme that offers tax advantages for investment in the appropriate sort of company.

10.2. Deferring Capital Gains by Reinvesting

10.2.1.   Enterprise Investment Scheme (EIS)

The **EIS** offers three forms of tax relief to an individual who invests in **new** shares in an EIS company:

- Income tax relief (at 30%) on the amount (generally up to £1,000,000 but the limit has increased to £2million for "knowledge-intensive company" share investments from 6 April 2018) invested in EIS shares, provided that the individual is not "connected" with the company – that is, he and his "associates" do not own or control more than 30% of it.

- If the shares qualify for the above income tax relief, and they are later sold at a loss, that loss can be deducted from the investor's income for the year.

- If the shares qualify for the income tax relief, and are sold at a profit after more than three years, the profit is exempt from CGT, except for any gains "deferred" – see next bullet point.

- Deferral of other capital gains on **any amount** reinvested in EIS shares – this relief applies whether or not the individual is "connected" to the EIS company, and is the one we shall concentrate on here.

    The investment must be made within the same time limit as for rollover relief – one year before to three years after the gain to be deferred.

An EIS company must meet certain conditions if it is to be a "qualifying company" and its shareholders can get tax relief on their investment.

The detailed rules are very complicated, and expert tax advice is essential if you are contemplating an EIS investment, but in outline:

- The company must not be listed on a Stock Market

- It must not be controlled by another company

- It must carry on a "qualifying trade" and have a "permanent establishment" in the UK

A qualifying trade is defined by excluding certain types of trade – any other trade will be a "qualifying trade".

The following are **"excluded activities"** and a company which carries on any of these trades will **not** be a "qualifying company" for EIS purposes:

- Dealing in land, commodities, shares or other financial instruments

- Dealing in goods (except for ordinary wholesalers and retailers)

- Banking, insurance, money-lending, and other financial activities

- Leasing or receiving royalties or licence fees

- Providing legal or accountancy services

- **Property development** (before you get any ideas..!)

- Farming or market gardening

- Woodlands or forestry activities

- Shipbuilding

- Producing coal or steel

- Running hotels or similar establishments

- Running nursing homes or residential care homes

- Subsidised electricity generation

The EIS company must carry on its qualifying trade for at least three years from the date it issues the EIS shares on which tax relief is claimed.

The list of "excluded activities" means that a property company could never be an EIS company, but an EIS company investment may nevertheless be of interest to a property investor who has made a large capital gain by selling one or more of his properties.

Case Study - 18   EIS Deferral Relief

Gary has just sold his property portfolio for £2 million, and has made a gain of £500,000.

He decides to set up an eligible trading company. His Tax Adviser explains that it should be possible to set the company up in such a way that he will qualify for EIS deferral relief.

Gary pays his new company £500,000 and the company issues shares to him in return. Because Gary owns more than 30% of the company (in fact, he owns it all!) he cannot claim the EIS income tax relief on his subscription for the shares, but he can still claim deferral relief for his capital gain.

As Gary has invested the full amount of the gain in the EIS company, all of his capital gain is deferred – **note that for the EIS it is not necessary to invest all the sale proceeds, which is the case with rollover relief above, but just the gain itself.**

The company spends the £500,000 on setting up a trade (it must do this within strict time limits). Provided it continues to run the trade for at least three years, Gary's deferral relief is safe.

When Gary sells the shares, the £500,000 gain he deferred becomes taxable again – though he could defer the gain once more by investing in another EIS company.

Any gain on the shares themselves will not be exempt (because he did not qualify for the income tax relief as he owned over 30% of the company), but this too could be deferred by another EIS investment.

11. Some Property Tax Pitfalls

In this chapter we will look at one or two pitfalls that the property business owner should be aware of.

One of these concerns a property investment partnership, and the other a company.

11.1. Partnerships?

We have already seen in section 1.2 of this guide that a partnership is "persons carrying on a business in common and with a view of profit".

The Partnership Act 1890 defines a "business" as including "every trade, occupation or profession".

HMRC takes the view that simply owning a property jointly with another person and receiving a share of the rent from it does not amount to an "occupation or profession", and we have already seen that it is not a trade.

They argue that in most cases, income from jointly owned property is not income from a partnership.

11.1.1. Why Does It Matter?

Given that HMRC accepts that joint owners of property can agree how the income from the property is divided between them, this distinction may not seem very important.

In the case of joint owners of property who are not married, the distinction is unlikely to become relevant unless one of them is also a partner in a trading business which itself lets property, and then only if there are losses involved:

Case Study - 19   Partnerships (1)

Peter is a partner in a firm of tax advisers. The firm also owns a couple of investment properties, which it lets out. For the tax year 2018/19, the rentals from these properties produce a loss, of which Peter's share is £1,000.

Peter also owns a rental property jointly with his brother. During the same tax year, they make a profit on the rent from the property of £1,000 each.

Peter cannot set the loss from the partnership rents against the profit on the jointly owned property, because they are two separate property businesses, owned in different legal "capacities" – one as a joint owner, the other as a partner.

Bigger problems can arise, however, with rental properties jointly owned by a married couple (or a civil partnership).

This is because there is specific legislation (ITA 2007 s 836/7) that allocates the income from jointly owned assets to them, as follows:

- The income is deemed to be split equally between the couple, UNLESS

- They do not in fact own equal shares of it, and they elect (using a "Form 17")

- To be taxed based on their ACTUAL ownership of it.

Case Study - 20   Partnerships (2)

Rowley and his wife Nellie jointly own a property. Rowley pays income tax at 40%, but Nellie does not have any income. The rental profit from the property is £12,000 per year.

It seems sensible to the couple (who believe, wrongly, that they are a property letting partnership), to agree that the profits of the partnership should be split 10% to Rowley, and 90% to Nellie.

The tax inspector explains to them that in his opinion their property letting is not a partnership, because it does not involve sufficient business activity on their part – it is essentially a passive investment.

After some argument, they reluctantly accept his view, but Nellie asks why it is so important, given that HMRC accept that joint owners can agree how to divide the income from their property.

The inspector explains that this does not apply to married couples, and runs through the rules referred to above. Because the income from the jointly owned property must be split equally between them, the result is:

	Rowley	Nellie	Total
Rental split as "partnership"	1,200	10,800	12,000
Tax due	480	nil	480
Rental split 50:50	6,000	6,000	12,000
Tax due	2,400	nil	2,400

As a result of splitting the income in the correct way, the couple are paying £1,920 more income tax.

What could they do?

For the future, they could change their ownership of the property, by converting their joint ownership into a "tenancy in common" (a simple legal procedure), and

Rowley could then give 4/5 of his half share to Nellie (there is no CGT on gifts between spouses – but see next).

They would then own the property in a 90:10 proportion, and they could then submit a Form 17 to the inspector, but the new split of the income would apply only from the date they made this "declaration". Furthermore, they still do not have the flexibility of co-owners who are not married to each other / in a civil partnership.

11.2. SDLT Implications Of Transfers Involving A Mortgage

Note that if there is a mortgage on the property, then a gift between spouses may give rise to a charge to Stamp Duty Land Tax (SDLT) and, even if it does not, the gift must be notified to HMRC on Form SDLT1.

Case Study - 21   Gifts and Stamp Duty

A husband owns a buy to let property valued at £300,000, on which he has secured a mortgage of £240,000. He makes a gift of the property (still encumbered with the mortgage), to his wife.

Although the wife did not pay anything for the property, she has taken over responsibility for the £240,000 mortgage, so she must pay SDLT of £9,500 including the additional 3% charge. (Note that with the new rates introduced in April 2016, a married couple may have only one 'exempt main residence' between them. This is a significant increase on the pre-April 2016 rates, where the cost would have been as little as £2,300.)

If instead the husband had only given her a half share in the property, she would normally be treated as having taken over half the mortgage, being £120,000 (practically, it is the mortgage lenders who would want her to take on the responsibility). This would now cost £3,600 in SDLT, but before April 2016 it would have been SDLT-free, although there would still have been a duty to notify HMRC using Form SDLT1.

11.3. SDLT, Partnerships And Incorporation

There is a possible charge to SDLT on the incorporation of a property business – and it is potentially very large, since it applies to the market value of the property/ies. It doesn't matter if the company pays nothing for the portfolio, because the trigger is simply a transfer between individuals and a company with which they are "connected" – basically, in which they are shareholders. As regards residential properties, the SDLT rate can be as high as 15% - but companies can avail themselves of either Multiple Dwellings Relief, or – when buying 6 or more dwellings – the cheaper commercial (non-residential) property rates. For more information on these reliefs, please see our report **"Incorporating a Property Business"**

Partnerships (and Limited Liability Partnerships) *may* be able to avoid an SDLT charge entirely, however, thanks to specific provisions that reduce the charge when such bodies incorporate. Simple joint investments are ineligible – it cannot be a passive investment but rather an active partnership business. Businesses that think they may be eligible for partnership treatment should take detailed advice on the matter beforehand, as property businesses are liable to challenge.

Individuals should also beware creating a partnership (or LLP) in order to try to circumvent the SDLT charge on subsequent incorporation of the new partnership: there is SDLT anti-avoidance legislation that will "ignore" transactions or arrangements that (loosely) are undertaken to secure a lower SDLT charge.

11.4. Increased SDLT Risk For Companies – Indecision Costs Money!

Where a company purchases a single dwelling property costing more than £500,000, then it is **potentially** exposed to a 15% SDLT rate on the whole consideration, **unless** the company is to use it for:

- A property rental business, or
- A property development business

(Certain other dwellings are excluded, such as farmhouses and properties used by employees or made available to the public).

This means that BTL landlords and property developers operating through companies should be safe from the increased SDLT charge, but perhaps one thing you should NOT say to your conveyancing solicitor when he asks what your company intends to do with the new £500,000+ property it has just purchased is "I don't know / I haven't decided yet"!

With regard to the 3% SDLT surcharge on additional residential properties, the maximum SDLT rate is not 15%+3% but only 15%. Note that companies cannot have a main residence that they can replace to avoid the 3% charge, so it will generally fall due on **every** property purchase, including the first. However, there are measures that companies (and other property buyers) can employ to reduce their SDLT exposure when acquiring several residential properties together, such as:

- Multiple Dwellings Relief when acquiring more than one dwelling at a time, and
- The lower non-residential/commercial property SDLT rates when acquiring 6 or more residences together

11.5. Annual Tax On "Enveloped Dwellings" (ATED)

Just in case a potential 15% SDLT charge on acquisition were not enough, there is also an Annual Tax on Enveloped Dwellings. "Enveloped dwellings" basically means dwellings that are held in a company, or similar arrangement. ATED applies only to high-value dwellings that are individually worth more than £500,000. Here again, relief is available from ATED for dwellings that are used in:

- A property rental business, or
- A property development business

But relief from ATED must be claimed, so property companies have to submit a Relief Declaration Return covering their let properties, (and/) or a different Relief Declaration Return covering development properties. The deadline is usually 30 April every year, but it may be a different date for the first period in which the company has to claim the relief. There are penalties if the claims are submitted late.

Ordinary BTL properties will count as "dwellings" but hotels, guest houses, care homes and student halls of residence should not.

One or two aspects of ATED to catch out the unwary:

- ATED is assessed by reference to the dwelling's value. Where recently acquired, the cost can be used for its value. However, properties have to be revalued periodically – April 2017 is the most recent valuation date, so properties may now be caught that were previously 'safe'.

- If a property is let to a person "connected" with the owner(s), such as to a relative of the company's shareholder(s), then ATED is chargeable: **even if the arrangements are by way of a normal rental agreement at a full market rate, the rental business relief (or, if relevant, the property development business relief) is not available**.

- If a high-value property is unused but is not being marketed or repaired, etc., then there is a risk that ATED will be triggered because it will fall outside the aforementioned relief, if only until it is active again.

- When the property is sold or there is otherwise a disposal for CGT purposes, then the company will be subject to ATED CGT if it was caught by the Annual Tax itself during the time it was owned. (A corresponding proportion of the gain arising is subject to ATED CGT). The rate for ATED CGT is 28% - even though ordinary corporate capital gains are taxed at the standard rate of 19%. See also Foreign Ownership, below.

The rules for ATED are complex, and people new to the regime should seek advice from a suitably qualified Tax Adviser. An ordinary BTL or property development company has little to fear from ATED, however, so long as it:

- Files its Relief Declaration Return(s) on time, as and when they are required
- Does not let connected individuals occupy its high-value properties
- Monitors its voids to ensure that high-value properties are actively managed in the business

11.6. Foreign Ownership

I have come across many property investors who think that holding UK property through an offshore vehicle – and/or perhaps becoming non-resident themselves – will somehow reduce their tax bill. We look at investing in overseas properties separately in Chapter 19, and many of the rules mentioned there apply also to offshore companies holding UK properties. While tax saving is not impossible, there are numerous aspects to consider, including the following:

If the individual and/or the company is not resident in the UK, then they are likely resident in another country / territory, and therefore subject to that territory's tax regime. Some territories do not tax the overseas income or gains of their residents, but most do – and some will tax more heavily than in the UK.

The UK's domestic tax code generally makes income from UK property taxable in the UK. Double Taxation Treaties with other countries may potentially override that rule but in fact, many Treaties actually do the opposite, and effectively allow **both** the territory where the property is, **and** the territory where the taxpayer is resident, to tax the same property income. (The UK will generally allow relief for foreign tax already paid on that income source, however, so this may not actually cost more tax).

A similar approach applies to an individual who is not resident in the UK but operates (say) a property development trade in the UK: the UK would still want to tax profits arising from the UK trading activity, as would, in all likelihood, the territory in which the individual was tax resident (subject to offset, as with rental profits). Furthermore, capital gains on any assets sold in the UK that were used in a UK trading activity would be subject to UK CGT, by default.

If a non-resident individual or company sells UK residential property, then it will be exposed to Non-Resident CGT (NRCGT) on the part of the gain deemed to arise since 5 April 2015, when the new regime was introduced. (There are exceptions for the main residence). NRCGT applies at the standard rates. A non-resident company could potentially be caught for ATED CGT (see above) AND NRCGT on the same UK property gain, in which case ATED CGT takes precedence (at a rate of 28%). Even if no NRCGT is due, an NRCGT return should still be filed within 30 days of conveyance, or penalties may be incurred. Where a property has been owned for a long time, however, the relatively new NRCGT regime may not turn out to be that expensive, however. The government intends to broaden the scope of the NRCGT regime to include commercial properties as well, from April 2019.

Case Study - 22   Non Resident CGT

Jean, who is resident in France, has a UK rental property, which he has owned since April 2002, when it cost him £250,000. It was worth £600,000 when the new NRCGT regime was introduced in April 2015, and he sold it for £650,000 in April 2017. ATED CGT is not in point, because the offshore owner is an individual.

	Default Calculation	Time-apportioned Calculation
Proceeds April 2017	650,000	650,000
Less: Value April 2015	(600,000)	
Less: Original Cost April 2002		(250,000)
	50,000	400,000
Proportion since April 2015 2 years since April 2015		53,333

15 years' total ownership period		
Use default option as lower gain	50,000	
Less: Annual Exemption (2017/18)	(11,300)	
Taxable Gain	**38,700**	

Jean has several possible calculation methods available to him.

The simplest – and default method – is to calculate the proceeds against the property's value when the new regime was introduced on 5 April 2015.

Alternatively, he can calculate the gain over the entire ownership period (since March 1982, if owned earlier) and tax the proportion of the resulting gain attributable to the period of ownership after April 2015. In this case, the default method results in a lower gain so Jean chooses the default basis.

If Jean had owned the property for a longer period overall, then the proportion of gain attributable to post-April 2015 could fall to a lower amount than that derived from the default basis, so Jean would plump for the time-apportionment basis. (There is a further alternative basis but it is rarely likely to be useful).

Jean may also be taxed in France on this gain!

It is quite difficult to 'keep' an offshore company offshore, if its directors are resident in the UK: if it is effectively managed in the UK then it may become UK tax resident even if originally constituted offshore. Can UK-based directors practically undertake their executive meetings and decisions offshore – and how expensive might that be?

There is a great deal of anti-avoidance legislation designed to attribute income or gains in an offshore company to its UK shareholders. Most recently, new rules have been introduced, basically to ensure that income derived from developing UK land or property is taxed as a trade in the UK, even if the entity that owns the property has no presence in the UK whatsoever.

Offshore taxation is extremely complex, not least because it has the potential to involve not just the UK tax regime but another country's tax code as well. It demands comprehensive advice from a specialist Tax Adviser.

11.7. How Limited is Your Liability?

One of the advantages of a company over a sole trade or a partnership is said to be the fact that the shareholder's liability is "limited" – see section 1.3 of this guide.

This is true as far as it goes, but in the real world, this "limited liability" can be an illusion.

A company needs cash. When it first starts its business life, it can raise that cash from only one or two sources:

- By issuing shares in exchange for cash

- By borrowing money

The cash shareholders put into the company when they subscribe for shares is, of course, at risk if things go wrong – "limited liability" means that at worst they will lose this money.

When a company borrows money, it can either borrow it from:

- Its shareholders, or

- Commercial lenders – such as banks

Clearly, if the money is borrowed from the shareholders, they are also at risk for that money if things go wrong (and note that if their company is in difficulties, there are strict rules against repaying shareholders' loans in preference to the company's other debts).

If the company borrows from a commercial lender (say, a bank), particularly when it is a fairly new company, it is extremely likely that the bank will demand a "personal guarantee" from one or more of the shareholders/directors.

A "personal guarantee" (known as a "PG") is a promise from the individual concerned that if the company fails to repay the money it has borrowed, then the individual will step in and repay the loan himself.

Typically, a PG will be backed up by a "charge" on the individual's other property – most typically, his home. A "charge" means that if the individual fails to repay the loan after the company defaults, then the bank can take his home and sell it to get its money back.

In many cases, therefore, the limited liability offered by a company will not be as good a protection as it may appear at first sight:

Case Study - 23   Limited Liability

Andrew sets up a company to develop a property. The company needs £250,000 to buy the property and to renovate it and sell it. The money comes from:

- Andrew's subscription for shares - £10,000

- Loan from Andrew (his life savings) - £40,000

- Loan from High Street Bank (with a PG from Andrew) - £200,000

The company buys the land and begins to develop it, but unfortunately discovers that there are old mine workings undermining the entire property.

Building work cannot continue, and the land is sold off at a knock-down price (being virtually useless for anything). When the dust settles, the company's assets are £100,000 in cash.

Because the £100,000 is not enough to repay the bank, they call in Andrew's PG (which is secured on his house), and he has to sell this in order to pay the £100,000 owed to the bank after it has taken all the company's cash.

Andrew also loses the £40,000 he had lent to the company, and his £10,000' worth of shares are now worth nothing. Andrew does not feel that his limited liability as a shareholder has been much help to him!

In certain other circumstances, a director may become liable for the company's debts even though he has not lent it any money, nor given any PGs.

If a director allows a company to continue in business when he knows (**or should have known**) that the company will not be able to pay its debts, then he can be sued for "wrongful trading", and can be required to provide funds to help the company pay off its creditors.

For this reason, directors whose companies are getting into financial trouble should not ignore the problem. They should seek their accountant's advice immediately, in order to avoid the risk of becoming personally liable if the company goes under.

12. Close Companies

All of the companies featured in the case studies in this guide are "close" companies. In this chapter we will become more familiar with this terminology and understand what it means.

12.1. What is a Close Company?

A "close" company is a company that is controlled by:

- Five or fewer "participators", or

- Any number of "participators", if those "participators" are also directors

A "participator", broadly, means a shareholder although loan creditors may, in some circumstances, also be participators.

Case Study - 24   Examples of Close Companies

Example of "close" companies include:

- The shares in Company A are owned equally by three individuals. Company A is a close company, because it is controlled by five or fewer participators

- The shares in Company B are owned **equally** by nine individuals. Company B is a close company, because any five out of the nine could control it

- The shares in company C are owned equally by five married couples. Company C is a close company, because when looking at "control" you include shares held by "associates" and spouses are associates of each other.

- The shares in company D are owned by ten directors who each hold 10% of the company's shares. Even though it would generally require six of those directors to exercise control, the company is still close because they are all directors of the company as well.

This is only a very broad summary of the rules defining a close company, because the detailed rules are extremely complicated, being designed to prevent people artificially creating a company which should be a close company but is not.

For the purposes of this guide, assume that any property investment or property development company you set up is going to be a close company.

12.2. Special Rules for Close Companies

There are certain special rules for close companies, which cover:

- The meaning of a "distribution" from the close company

- The tax on loans from the close company to its participators

- The way corporation tax is calculated for certain types of close company

12.3. The Meaning of a "Distribution" From a Close Company

If a close company provides any "benefits or facilities of whatever nature" to a participator (or his associates) in a close company, then this is treated as if the company had paid him a dividend equivalent to the benefit.

This does not apply if the participator is also a director or employee of the company, where the benefit will be charged to income tax as part of his remuneration from the company. It is therefore quite unusual to come across this alternative dividend scenario:

Case Study - 25   Distribution to a Participator

Closeco Ltd is a close company, and Daniel is one of the shareholders. Daniel is not a director and does not work for the company, and is not related to any of the other shareholders. The company manufactures TV sets, and one Christmas, it gives each of its shareholders a brand new plasma TV.

Most of the shareholders are directors of the company and so they are taxed on the TVs as a benefit in kind from their employment, but Daniel is not, so he is treated as if he had received a dividend equivalent to the cost to the company of the TV.

If the cost of the TV is £1,000, then Daniel (a higher rate taxpayer) will be charged to income tax of £325.

The company is able to claim a deduction for the cost of the TVs supplied to the directors (as a cost of employing them), but it cannot get a deduction for the cost of Daniel's TV.

12.4. Loan To Participator

Much more common is a **loan to a participator**.

This will occur if the company lends money to one of its shareholders. The company will be required to pay tax under section 455 CTA 2010 on the amount of the loan (hence the nickname "section 455 tax"). For loans made on or after 6 April 2016, the rate of tax is 32.5% of the amount of the loan (for many years before that date, the rate was 25%).

When the loan is repaid, the tax will be refunded. The timing of this is important.

Case Study - 26   Section 455 Tax

A close company makes a loan of £10,000 to a shareholder. When it puts in its corporation tax return (which must be within nine months after its year-end), it must include section 455 tax of £3,250 in its tax payment – unless the loan is repaid within nine months of the end of that accounting period, in which case no section 455 tax is due. If, for example, 60% of the loan is repaid in time, then only 40% of the section 455 tax actually be payable.

Assuming the loan is **not** repaid within nine months of the end of the accounting period in which it was made, then the section 455 tax will be due in full and will only be repaid nine months after the end of the accounting period in which the loan is actually repaid. (The same approach applies to part-repayments made after the initial nine-month deadline).

For example:
The company prepares its accounts for the calendar year, and on 31 December 2017 it lends £10,000 to a shareholder. The loan is repaid on 1 January 2019 – just over 12 months later (but, importantly, this is the *second* accounting period after the loan was actually made – the loan was outstanding for all of the accounting period ended 31 December 2018).

On 1 October 2018, the company pays its corporation tax for the 2017 year, and section 455 tax of £3,250.

On 1 October 2019, the company pays its corporation tax for the 2018 return year. It cannot yet claim back any section 455 tax, because although the loan has been repaid by now, it was repaid after the end of the 2018 return year.

On 1 October 2020, the company pays its corporation tax for the 2019 year, and because it is now nine months after the end of the accounting period in which the loan was repaid, it can claim repayment of the section 455 tax.

Although the loan was only outstanding for one year and two days at the most, the section 455 tax is not repaid until two years after it was paid.

Some companies try to get around this by "bed and breakfasting" the loan:

The company makes up its accounts to the calendar year. On 1 January 2018, it lends £40,000 to a shareholder.

On 30 December 2018, the shareholder borrows £40,000 from his rich uncle, and repays the loan.

On 2 January 2019, he again borrows £40,000 from the company, and repays his uncle.

On 30 December 2019, he borrows £40,000 from uncle… and so on!

Because the loan never appears in the company's balance sheet at 31 December, the company believes there is no section 455 tax to pay – after all, the loan has been repaid, hasn't it?

HMRC take the view that a temporary repayment of a loan in this way is not effective – it is very unwise for a company to rely on "bed and breakfasting" a loan in this way.

Legislation in CTA 2010 s 464 (as amended by FA 2013) specifically targets this practice of "bed and breakfasting" loans. Depending on the size of the loan, the repayment is ignored (so the section 455 tax remains due) if it takes place less than 30 days before a further loan (loans over £5,000), or if there are "arrangements" for a further loan at the time of the repayment (loans over £15,000). HMRC may, however, allow amounts made out of salary or dividend credited to the participator's loan account, rather than having been paid out to him directly.

In order to get the section 455 tax repaid, the company can also write off the loan. In other words, the company formally declares that it will cancel the loan. The tax consequences of this are:

- The company can claim repayment of the section 455 tax as if the loan had been repaid (or if the loan is written off within 9 months of the accounting period in which it was made, no section 455 tax will be due).

- The shareholder is taxed as if he had received a dividend equal to the loan being written off.

This can be used as a planning tool:

Case Study - 27   Write off of a Loan

In Case Study 11, we saw the problems that can arise if a company pays dividends to its shareholders that are not proportionate to their shareholdings. If instead of paying a dividend to the shareholders, the company lent them money and then wrote off the loan, they would get the same tax effect as a dividend.

The timing of the tax payment can be better, as well. Compare the timing of the tax payment between a dividend and a loan written off:

The company makes up its accounts to the calendar year.

In scenario A, it pays a dividend of £5,000 on 6 April 2018 to a shareholder, who pays income tax at the higher rate and has already used his new Dividend Allowance from other sources.

In scenario B, it lends £5,000 to the same shareholder, also on 6 April 2018. It then writes the loan off on 6 April 2019 (i.e., less than 9 months after its year-end of 31 December 2018).

In scenario A, the shareholder has received a dividend in the tax year 2018/19. He will be liable to pay income tax of £1,625 by 31 January 2020.

In scenario B, the shareholder is deemed to have received a distribution (dividend) in the tax year 2019/20 (the tax year in which the loan was written off, not the tax in which the loan was originally made). He will be liable to pay the same amount of income tax (£1,625), but not until 31 January 2021.

Because the loan was written off within 9 months of the end of the accounting year in which it was made, the company does not have to pay any section 455 tax. In both scenarios, the shareholder has had the use of the money from 6 April 2016, but the date on which he has to pay income tax on it has been deferred by a year.

Caution

This particular planning technique is not as simple as it appears, and you should take advice from a Tax Adviser before using it. There are a number of aspects of company law to consider, and also the "preordained series of transactions" rules we have already looked at – see Case Study - 15. There may also be problems with NIC and taxable benefits in kind, if the shareholder is also a director.

13. The Directors' Tax Liabilities

So far, we have looked only at the tax that directors of a company will pay on salaries and dividends.

This chapter considers the other tax liabilities they may have in relation to the company.

13.1. Tax on Non-Cash Benefits

Directors (and other employees) are liable to tax on non-cash benefits they receive from the company that employs them. We shall refer only to "directors" in this book for simplicity.

The whole area of employee benefits is a complex and specialised branch of tax, but this chapter attempts to give some guidelines on the pitfalls to avoid, and one or two opportunities as well.

Directors are also potentially liable to tax on any business expenses that the company reimburses to them, (but not if they were incurred for business purposes, generally speaking – i.e., the potential benefit of a reimbursement is cancelled out if the director can claim a business purpose for his or her expense).

13.2. Expenses

Directors may incur expenses when on the company's business. The most common example is travelling expenses.

13.2.1. Travelling expenses

The cost of business travel is an allowable expense, subject to certain exclusions. The one that most commonly causes problems is travel from home to work.

Travel from your home to your normal place of work is "ordinary commuting" and the cost is NOT allowable as a business expense. This can be a particular problem for the typical small family company.

If the company has a headquarters, such as a rented office in a town, or a yard where it keeps its building equipment, then travel from home to that place is unlikely to be an allowable expense.

If, on the other hand, the company's base of operations is the home of the controlling director, travel from his home to anywhere that the company's business is being conducted – such as a building site, or a property being refurbished – is usually an allowable expense.

If a property investment company uses a letting agent to administer the properties it lets, then it is likely that HMRC will argue that the business is being administered through the agent, and that therefore the director's home is just a home, and not where the company's business is carried on, even if he brings paperwork home occasionally.

Any company whose directors are incurring significant travelling expenses should check with a Tax Adviser to confirm that the expenses are allowable – getting it wrong can be expensive, as we shall see in chapter 14, which deals with tax investigations.

13.2.2. Cars

Most travelling expenses involve the cost of running a car.

It used to be a good tax planning idea to have the company own a car, and to allow the director to use it for both business and private purposes, as the rules for taxing directors on their private use of a "company car" *used to be* quite generous.

These rules have been made progressively more punitive over the years, and it is now very unlikely that it will be beneficial for a director who also owns the company to have a company car.

There is no substitute for doing the figures for the individual director and car, but it nearly always turns out that he will be better off owning the car privately and charging the company for his business mileage, as below.

13.2.3. Using Your Own Car for Business

A director who uses his own car for business mileage can be reimbursed tax free by the company at a rate of 45p per mile for the first 10,000 business miles in the tax year (year to 5 April), and at 25p per mile for any further business mileage.

Note that this is now the only reimbursement that is allowable for employee tax purposes. If the director instead claims the actual cost of his business mileage from the company – by keeping records of all running costs and of his business and private mileage – then, when the company pays him for these expenses, the payment is taxable. Where amounts paid by the company are less than the HMRC-approved rates, then the difference can be reclaimed on your tax return.

13.2.4. Using Cars for Sole Traders and Partnerships

A sole trader or partner in a property business can keep full records and claim the actual cost of the business miles, or he can use the flat rate mileage allowances described above. (There are exceptions to this for high-turnover businesses – check with your Tax Adviser or accountant).

13.2.5. Three Important Differences to Remember

This is an excellent example of three important differences between the tax treatment of companies and their directors as compared to sole traders/partners:

- The relationship between a company and its director is more formal than that between a sole trader/partner and his business

- The rules for directors tend to be restrictive and punitive compared to sole traders

- The differences between the two sets of rules defy common sense!

13.3. Other Expenses

Motoring expenses, providing the rules described above are followed, are not taxable on directors, but many other expenses can be – for example:

- The company pays the director's train fare to visit a development site where the company is building some buy-to-sell properties

- The director has to attend a meeting to close a deal on a new property, and because it is a long journey from his home, the company reimburses him for the cost of an overnight stay in a hotel

- The director uses his own credit card to pay for goods or services for the company, and claims the cost back from the company

- The director takes herself and her spouse on a night out to celebrate finishing a challenging development project, spending £500 in total.

Following the abolition of "dispensations" in 2016, it is down to the employer to determine if an expense has been incurred for business purposes and may be considered non-taxable. Otherwise, it must be reported and will probably be taxable. Of the four examples above, it is clearly the last that is problematic. There are in fact reasonably generous provisions relating to annual staff events and 'trivial' benefits in kind but the cost in this case would exceed those thresholds, and would need to be reported to HMRC.

They must either be reported on the company's annual return of benefits provided to a director (known as a Form P11D) or, in the case of cash payments, they should strictly be paid under deduction of PAYE. Employers have the option now to "payroll" some benefits rather than use the P11D reporting system.

13.4. Shares as Rewards

We have seen how the company is owned by its shareholders, and how their shares entitle them to their proportion of dividends paid and, ultimately, to a share of the company's assets when it is wound up. For many years, shares have also been used as a way of providing benefits to employees, and in some cases as a way of trying to pay them in a way that escaped tax and NIC, or reduce their impact.

As a result, HMRC and the Treasury have introduced more and more complex and punitive rules taxing employees and directors on the benefit of any "employment related securities" (including shares) which they are given.

This is not the place for a detailed examination of these rules (that would take a book longer than the whole of this one) but the following Case Study illustrates the type of pitfall to watch out for.

Case Study - 28   Shares as Rewards

Mr Fox and Mr Hound each own very similar property development companies. They are both the sole shareholders, and they are both getting on in years.

Mr Fox has two sons, who both work in the business, and he decides he would like to give them 24% of his shares each – Mr Fox is a great family man, and says he believes in "keeping the family business within the family". He will still have 52% of the shares, but if all goes well over the next few years, he will be able to hand over full control and enjoy a well-earned retirement.

Mr Hound is in exactly the same situation and has exactly the same plans, except that in his case he has only one daughter, and no sons. He does, however, have a very loyal manager (not related to him and, though on good terms with the family, not a close friend), who has worked for the company for many years, and who could be trusted to help his daughter in running the company – "she has a good eye for property, and he is an excellent project manager", he explains. Mr Hound does exactly the same as Mr Fox – he gives 24% of his shares to each of his daughter and the manager, with a view to handing over to them entirely in a few years if all goes well.

Because Foxco Ltd and Houndco Ltd are both trading companies, Mr Fox and Mr Hound can "hold over" the capital gains tax on their disposals of their shares – which is just as well, because the shares are now worth several hundreds of thousands of pounds – both companies are doing well and have a number of profitable projects on the go.

The tax treatment of the <u>recipients</u> of the shares is very different, though.

In the Fox brothers' case, HMRC will probably accept that the gift of the shares is covered by the <u>ONLY</u> exception to the rules for "employment related securities", which excludes shares given to employees "in the normal course of the domestic, family, or personal relationships" of the person giving them.

There are no income tax implications for the Fox boys.

Miss Hound and the manager, however, are in a very different position. Because Miss Hound received her shares at the same time as the (unrelated) manager, it may be difficult to argue that hers were "domestic, family, or personal relationships" shares.

It certainly cannot be argued that the manager's shares were not in some way related to his job.

You will also notice that Mr Fox was careful to stress the importance of family, and to downplay the obvious fact that he hoped the boys would be motivated to put more effort into the company once they owned a large slice of it, whereas Mr Hound could not resist mentioning what a good job the manager <u>and his daughter</u> were doing.

As a result, Miss Hound and the manager are exposed to income tax on the market value (hundreds of thousands of pounds, remember!) of the shares they

> have been given and, in the particular circumstances of this case, there may even be a PAYE and NIC liability, which Houndco will have to pay, and then *further* tax liabilities if Miss Hound and the manager do not reimburse the company for that tax and NIC.
>
> If you think the distinction between the way the two companies were treated is exaggerated, please note that both Foxco and Houndco are based on real cases.

It is <u>never</u> safe to assume that if an employee or director (or their close family) acquires shares in the company he works for, then there will be no tax implications.

Even if **you** acquire your shares following the setting up your own new company, it is possible that the company will be required to report the fact (on a "Form 42", by 7 July after the end of the tax year in which you acquired the shares).

There are some narrow exceptions to this rule, but they are *very* narrow exceptions.

Always ask your Tax Adviser **before** you enter into **any** transaction involving shares and employees (including directors) – this is a complicated and 'dangerous' area, but to look on the bright side, there is much that can be done to reduce the tax burdens involved.

13.5. FOUR Tax Free Benefits

To end this Part on a more cheerful note, let us look at a few benefits that a company can provide to its directors without any tax liability arising.

The tax free benefits provided below may seem trivial, but their value mounts up.

Car Parking
The company can provide any employee with a car parking space at or near his place of work (either in the company's own car park, or in a commercial car park).

Mobile Phones
The company can provide a mobile phone – though since April 2006, this has been restricted to one phone per employee. Do **not** fall into the trap of simply reimbursing the director for his own, personal mobile contract and assuming that is the same thing – the latter is taxable and potentially NIC'able as well.

Child Care
The company can pay for childcare (in a commercial nursery or with an approved child-minder) for employees' children, up to a maximum of £55 per week per employee, free of tax. **This "childcare voucher" scheme is to be closed to new entrants from October 2018, so advice should be sought promptly if it may be of use!**

Note that this benefit must be offered to all employees, whereas the benefits mentioned previously may be offered selectively. Of course, this may not be problematic if the company has only one or two directors and no other employees.

The level of tax free childcare varies according to the amount of other income the individual concerned has from the company.

In theory, since 2011, this relief is restricted for higher earners, but the rules are ridiculously easy to avoid for a family company.

Meals

Provided they are available to all employees, free meals in a works canteen or in the business premises (e.g. sandwich lunches) are tax free, provided they are "on a reasonable scale" (so no caviar sandwiches!). Note that the exemption does not apply to meals in cafes, restaurants, or pubs.

Case Study - 29   Tax Free Benefits

Mr and Mrs Laurel have a property company. They are the directors, and there are no employees. The company provides them with the following benefits:

- A parking space each (they have two cars, and often one of them needs to go off alone, to visit a site for example) in the multi-storey near the company's office. The cost is £30 per week each

- A mobile phone each – cost £25 per month each

- Childcare for their two-year-old twins – cost £55 per week each

- Sandwich lunches eaten at their desks when they are in the office – cost £15 per week each

The total yearly cost of these benefits is £10,790 (based on 45 working weeks in the year in the case of the sandwiches). The company gets a tax deduction for all of these costs, so the actual cost is only £8,740 after taking account of the tax relief in the company.

Mr and Mrs Hardy have a similar company, and incur all the same expenses as those above, but they pay for them out of their (taxed) dividend income because they wrongly assume they would have to pay tax on benefits in kind if the company provided them.

In order to have £10,790 to spend on these expenses, they need to draw sufficient dividends from the company, on which they pay tax at 32.5%, so the total dividend required is £15,985 (remember, the company does not get a deduction for the cost of a dividend).

By using the company to pay expenses they would have incurred anyway, the Laurels have saved around £7,000. Director/shareholders should note, however, that these benefits should not be offered to any employee (directors included) alongside a cash alternative – HMRC has significantly tightened up on so-called "salary sacrifice arrangements" and, although childcare vouchers are protected, other benefits can be taxed as if the employee had received the cash alternative.

14. Companies and Tax Investigations

HMRC have the power to "enquire" into any tax return from a company, a partnership, or an individual. They do not have to give a reason for the enquiry.

These "enquiries" come in several different forms, and this Part concentrates on the types of enquiry a company may face.

A sole trader or partnership is just as likely to face an enquiry, but as we shall see in this chapter, there are certain special features when a company is involved.

14.1. "Aspect" Enquiries

These are the least serious type of Enquiry – though they have been known to develop into "Full Enquiries" as they progress.

In an Aspect Enquiry, the inspector will ask questions about a specific issue in the return – a favourite example for a property letting/investment company would be to check if amounts claimed for repairs to a let property are in fact improvements to it (that cannot be deducted from rental profits, although they may instead be allowed for CGT, when the property is sold, for example). A common query for property development companies would be whether or not projects in progress at the accounts year-end had been correctly valued, so as to recognise an appropriate level of profit.

Many Aspect Enquiries are closed down with no penalties being charged – though this is not always the case if large or blatant errors are found – but there will be interest to pay on any additional tax that is collected, running from the date the tax would have been paid if the return had been correct in the first place.

14.2. "Compliance" Enquiries

This is a term for Enquiries aimed at checking that the business has complied with its obligations under the various laws and regulations it is obliged to obey. For property businesses, the commonest are:

- **Construction Industry Scheme (CIS) compliance**
  The CIS applies to all property developers (but not normally to property investors – see section 7.3 above), and requires them to check the credentials of all the subcontractors they use, and record all payments to them, while in some cases deducting tax from those payments.

  See our other guide "**Tax Secrets for Property Developers and Renovators**" for more details of the CIS and the procedure for HMRC checks on compliance.

- **PAYE and benefits in kind**
  A sole trader or partnership will be liable to this type of Enquiry only if it has employees, but ANY company could face one – because its directors are employees for tax purposes.

  The Enquiry will check if the company has operated PAYE correctly, and if all benefits in kind and expenses payments have been correctly reported on the annual Forms P11D.

- **VAT**

HMRC will (for example) check that any property purchases have been handled correctly regarding Transfer of a Going Concern issues and that "options to tax" (charge VAT) have been exercised correctly on commercial buildings; for companies making both VAT'able and exempt supplies – common in companies dealing with both residential and commercial property – then VAT Partial Exemption calculations are likely to be scrutinised.

Finally, the Capital Goods Scheme applies to properties (potentially including developments) costing more than £250,000 before VAT; very simply, when you buy such a property and VAT is in point, then you may have to monitor how it is used for up to 10 years, to make sure you haven't over claimed VAT. This often catches out businesses that sell or let out commercial property (on which they have – quite understandably – reclaimed VAT on initial purchase), but where they neglected to opt to tax their interest in the property beforehand.

- **Business Records Inspections**
  HMRC also have the power to visit business premises and inspect the books and the business assets. They can do this either by prior arrangement, or if they get authorisation from the Tax Tribunal, they can turn up unannounced. Note that you only have to let them in if they have authorisation from the Tribunal – if the authorisation is only signed by a senior HMRC officer you can tell them to go away and make an appointment. (Strictly, you do not have to let them in even if they *have* been authorised by the Tax Tribunal, but you may be charged up to £300 as a civil penalty unless you have a good reason for the refusal).

14.3. Full Enquiry

This is the type of Enquiry that is generally referred to as a Tax Investigation, and it will involve the inspector looking at all the business accounts and records, and in some cases the private bank statements, etc., of the owners or directors. It may also involve some or all of the more specialised types of Enquiry referred to above.

This is not the place for a detailed examination of how to deal with a tax investigation, but there is one vital piece of advice – **do not attempt to deal with it yourself!** In particular, if you or your company receive a notice from the tax inspector to say he has decided to "Enquire" into your or your company's return, **seek professional help immediately –** in the first instance, from your accountant, though in serious cases he may well want to call in tax specialists like us.

There are two specific problem areas in investigations that are peculiar to companies (though the first could also apply to a sole trader or partnership if they had employees):

14.4. "Grossing up"

Where an employee (including a director) has received payments that should have been made under PAYE, the inspector will generally argue that the tax liability should be settled by the employer rather than the employee, and that this should be done by "grossing up" the payments made.

Case Study - 30   Grossing Up

A company has paid a weekly cash sum of £50 to its directors to cover "general expenses". It is agreed that this "round sum payment" should have been paid under PAYE.

The directors are higher rate taxpayers, so for each director to have received £50 in cash, the PAYE deductions would have been:

Gross payment	85
Less income tax at 40%	(34)
Less employee's NIC at 2%	(1)
Gives weekly cash	50

In addition, the company would have had to pay employers' NIC at 13.8% on the £85 – another £11.

So, for each director involved, the annual amount of tax and NIC the inspector will seek to claim **for each year under enquiry** will be:

Weekly income tax	34
Weekly employee NIC	1
Weekly employer's NIC	11
Weekly total	46
Times 52 gives	2,392

(Note – the PAYE year is sometimes 53 weeks long, and also note it is HMRC practice to round down to the nearest pound)

"Grossing up" does not always happen – but it is almost always the position HMRC starts from, and you will need a Tax Adviser who has experience of negotiating with HMRC on these cases to ensure the damage is limited as much as possible.

14.5. Company Investigation Settlements

Company Investigation Settlements are also complicated by the way that companies and their directors are regarded by HMRC when it is found that tax has been lost, particularly as a result of undeclared income.

Case Study - 31   Undeclared Income in a Company

Mr Burke is a sole trader, and when his return and accounts are investigated, it is found that he has failed to include £10,000 income for the year – the rent from a property he owns.

The inspector explains that Mr Burke should have paid £4,000 income tax on this income, and so Mr Burke will have to pay:

Tax	4,000
Interest for late payment (say)	200
Penalties at 35% of tax (see later in this Part)	1,400
Total	5,600

(in reality, it is also likely that the £10,000 would be "scaled back" to the previous six years, perhaps using the Retail Price Index to estimate how much was missing in those years, but this has been ignored for the sake of simplicity)

Mr Burke agrees to this, pays up, and that is the end of the matter. Now let's look at a similar situation but this time in a company.

Mr Hare is the sole shareholder and director of a company, and it is found that £10,000 rental income has gone missing from his company's accounts and found its way into his pocket.

The tax consequences are more complicated, because HMRC take the view that sums "misappropriated" by directors are loans to them from the company.

This means that:

- The company has "lent" Mr Hare £10,000, and HMRC will insist that he pays it back as a condition of settling the Enquiry. If Mr Hare does not have the money, then the company may have to pay him a dividend to fund the repayment – income tax for Mr Hare of £3,250 (assuming his Dividend Allowance has already been used)

- The company owes section 455 tax (see Case Studies 25 and 26) of £3,250. Although this will be repaid when Mr Hare repays the "loan", the company will still have to pay interest on it from the date the company should have paid the section 455 tax.

- By lending the money interest-free to Mr Hare, the company has given him a benefit in kind, and he will have to pay income tax based on the official rate of interest (2.5% currently), so Mr Hare is taxed on a benefit of £300) – but this normally only runs from the date he agrees that the cash has been misappropriated until the day he repays it.

- The company should have paid corporation tax at 19% on the £10,000, so it owes £1,900

- As with Mr Burke, there will be interest and penalties on all this.

I have not offered a total of Mr Hare's and his company's costs, because these are so much a matter for negotiation with HMRC that any figure given could be misleading.

Note also that the "scaling back" to earlier years referred to with Mr Burke could apply here as well, so the amount Mr Hare will have to repay to the company could be very large indeed.

I have mentioned penalties, and it is important to understand how these are calculated, because it is possible to reduce them if the investigation is properly handled.

Penalty calculations start from the amount of the tax that has been wrongly underpaid – this is generally the maximum possible penalty, although things can be worse if there is an offshore aspect.

The actual penalty depends on:
- whether the taxpayer disclosed the error before HMRC enquired into his affairs
- whether the omission was "careless", "deliberate" or "deliberate and concealed"
- how helpful the taxpayer is in quantifying the tax lost

The rates of penalty for these various levels of misbehaviour are:

	Prompted disclosure	Mistake despite reasonable care	Failure to take reasonable care	Deliberate understatement	Deliberate understatement with concealment
1.	Max	0%	30%	70%	100%
2.	Min: Prompted	0%	15%	35%	50%
3.	Max reduction for prompted (1. – 2.)	0%	15%	35%	50%

	Unprompted disclosure	Mistake despite reasonable care	Failure to take reasonable care	Deliberate understatement	Deliberate understatement with concealment
4.	Max	0%	30%	70%	100%
5.	Min:	0%	0%	20%	30%
6.	Max reduction for prompted (4. – 5.)	0%	30%	50%	70%

Mr Burke had failed to declare £10,000 income (by not declaring rent he received from a property). The level of his penalties was agreed as 35%, on the basis that this was a "deliberate understatement", but he did not then attempt to conceal it and he cooperated in reaching a settlement

14.6. Watch Out for the Contractual Disclosure Facility (CDF) and COP 9

There is one other kind of investigation to consider. This is where HMRC believe there has been serious tax fraud. In these cases, they will send you a **Contractual Disclosure Form** under **Code of Practice 9 ("COP 9").**

If you are ever sent a CDF, it is **ABSOLUTELY ESSENTIAL** to take expert advice **immediately**. **UNDER NO CIRCUMSTANCES** try to handle this yourself, and, at the risk of offending the profession, it is unlikely that your regular accountant will have the expertise to deal with a CDF investigation.

14.7. Four Golden Rules of Tax Investigations

To end this part, here are the golden rules for dealing with tax enquiries:

- DON'T try to handle it yourself – get advice before you reply to the initial letter from the inspector, and at all costs DON'T ring the inspector up to "have a chat and sort this out"

- DON'T ignore it and hope it will go away – remember the mitigation of penalties for co-operation

- DO be honest and upfront with your Tax Adviser – only then will he be able to help you

- DO talk to your accountant about taking out insurance to cover the fees for a tax investigation – the professional fees can be very expensive

15. Getting Your Exit Strategy Right

It seems appropriate to include this towards the end of this guide, but in fact, **you should be thinking about your proposed exit route from the first day you start your business,** as it may affect how you set it up and the strategic decisions you make as time goes on.

15.1. Everybody Has an Exit Strategy

Some businessmen say they have no exit route – they will work till they drop, and leave the business to their children – but that is itself an exit route, and one we shall consider further in chapter 16.

15.2. The THREE Most Common Exit Strategies

If you decide not to leave the business to your children then it is highly likely you will adopt one of the following three possible exit routes:

- Sell the business as a going concern

- Liquidate the business and invest the cash in something else

- Keep the business as a source of retirement income

15.3. Selling the Business

For the sole trader or partner, there is little distinction between selling the business as a going concern, and simply selling off the business assets. In either case, he will pay capital gains tax on the gain he makes from the sale of the business assets, and his main concern will be whether or not he gets entrepreneurs' relief.

For a company, there will be a choice to make between:

- Selling the shares in the company

- The company sells its assets and the cash balance is then extracted from the company

It often happens that the decision is made for the company, because the purchaser insists either on buying the shares, or on buying the assets.

A purchaser will probably be thinking along these lines:

15.3.1. Benefits of Buying the Shares in the Company

- Simplicity – the company is already up and running and all he has to do is take it over. If the business name is important, buying the company is the simplest way to acquire the name (though this can be managed in other ways if assets are purchased).

- Stamp Duty – there is a flat rate of 0.5% for purchases of shares, whereas the Stamp Duty Land Tax on the purchase of land and property can be as high as 5% - or 15%, in the case of residential property.

- Financing – particularly if the purchaser is a listed company, it can offer its own shares in exchange for the shares in the business – more on this later.

15.3.2. Drawbacks of Buying the Shares in the Company

- History - when you buy a company's shares, you buy its history, including any skeletons it may have in its closet – for example, if the company has been getting its PAYE wrong, the problem will become yours once you own the shares, including any liabilities for years before you bought it.

  It is for this reason that Sale Agreements for companies tend to be more complicated than those for business assets alone, because they will (or should!) contain complex "warranties" (essentially, promises by the vendor that the company has no skeletons in the closet) and "indemnities" (promises by the vendor to pay for the funerals of any skeletons that do turn up after all!).

- Tax – in some circumstances, the purchaser may be able to get more tax reliefs for his purchase if he buys assets rather than the company – to take only one example, if a company buys business assets (not shares in a company) that include certain intangible assets, the company may be able to   get   a   tax deduction for the cost.

- Structure – if the purchaser already has a company, he may not want to buy another; if he does *not* already have a company, he may not want to run the business as a company.

From the vendor's point of view, there is a different set of considerations:

15.3.3. Benefits of Selling the Shares in the Company

- "Clean break" – by selling the company, he gets rid of its history – though this is subject to the warranties and indemnities he will probably have to give.

- CGT – especially if the shares qualify for entrepreneurs' relief, it is likely that he will pay less tax than if the company (which cannot claim entrepreneurs' relief) sells the assets.

- Double taxation – assuming the vendor wants the cash for himself, there is a "double whammy" if the company sells its business and is then liquidated, because the company will pay tax on the capital gains it makes on the sale of the assets, and then there will be another tax cost in extracting the funds from the company.

15.3.4. Benefits of Selling the Company's Assets and then Liquidating

I am tempted to say, "none", but it is always worth working the numbers for each individual case just to make sure.

The most common reason for asset sales is that the purchaser insists on it.

15.4. Selling the Company's Shares

Sale of company's shares. The basic proposition is quite simple – the shareholder(s) of the company sell their shares, and they make a capital gain based on the difference between the price they sell for, and the cost of those shares when they subscribed for them (typically very low – maybe even £1), or otherwise acquired them.

If the company is a trading company, they may get entrepreneurs' relief, and the effective rate of tax they pay on the sale may be as low as 10%; otherwise (as with a property investment company), they will pay CGT at 20%.

The reality, of course, is much more complicated, and it is essential to bring in a Tax Adviser at an early stage in all but the very simplest of company sales.

It is impossible to set out the "correct" strategy for selling a company.

Each company sale will have its own unique features, opportunities, and problems.

What follows are some examples of the kinds of situations that commonly arise:

15.4.1. "Earn-outs"

These are a very common feature of company sales. Essentially, the shares are sold for a cash sum up front, and with the promise of more cash depending on the company's performance over, say, the next three years. Points to consider with "earn-outs" include:

- Taxation of the earn-out. This can be complicated. If the deferred payments are fixed, such as "£100,000 on 31 March 2018, and £100,000 on 31 March 2019", then for tax purposes the vendor will be treated as receiving the **whole sum on the day he sells the company**.

  There are provisions for the CGT to be paid by instalments, and for repayments of CGT if the earn-out is never actually paid.

  If the deferred payments are uncertain at the time the company is sold – such as "40% of the profits made by the company in the next two years" – the treatment is different.

  The right to these future payments has to be valued at the time of the sale, and this value is taxed as part of the sale proceeds.

When and if the earn-out payments are made, the vendor is taxed on the difference between the value originally ascribed to the earn-out, and the amount then received.

Case Study - 33   Taxation of Uncertain Earn-Out

Sam sells his trading company for £200,000 cash up front, and 40% of the profits of the company in the year after the sale, payable four months after the end of that year when the accounts are signed off.

For the last three years the company's profits have averaged £250,000, so if all goes well, Sam expects to receive £100,000 for the earn-out. The cost of Sam's shares was a nominal £1, as he started the company himself from scratch three years ago.

It is agreed with HMRC that at the time of the sale, the value of the right to 40% of next year's profits, payable in 16 months' time, is £60,000. (This valuation takes account of both the fact that the amount of the payment is uncertain, and that Sam will have to wait for his money). On the sale of the company, Sam's CGT computation looks like this:

Sale cash	200,000
Value of earn-out	60,000
Total gain	260,000
CGT (after ER)	26,000

16 months later, it turns out that the company's profits were £200,000 for the year, so Sam's earn-out payment is £80,000.

His tax computation looks like this:

Payment received	80,000
Less value of earn-out	(60,000)
Taxable gain	20,000

Note that Sam gets no entrepreneurs' relief on the additional £20,000 – it is not a qualifying asset.

15.4.2. *"Employment-Related Shares or Securities"*

If the vendor is required to stay on as a director of the company for the earn-out period, as often happens so that he can "hand over the reins" to the new owners (and make sure his earn-out is as big as possible!), great care needs to be taken to make sure that he does not fall foul of the rules on "employment related securities" – see case Study - 27.

If the earn-out is paid in the form of loan notes or shares there is a danger that these will be treated as chargeable to income tax (on their market value) rather than to CGT – again, there are potentially ways around this, with good tax advice on the specific circumstances

15.4.3. *Payments Under Warranties and Indemnities*

The vendor often has to agree to pay the purchaser some sort of compensation if the company turns out not to be worth as much as he was told, or if there are unexpected tax liabilities.

It is important that the Sale Agreement is so worded that these are treated as refunds of the purchase price so that the vendor can get a CGT repayment, and the purchaser is not taxed on the payment until he eventually sells the shares.

15.4.4. *"Compensation for Loss of Office"*

There is an exemption from income tax and NIC for up to £30,000 paid to an employee who is sacked or made redundant, and Sale Agreements for companies quite often include provisions for £30,000 to be paid to the vendor (if he is expected to resign from his directorship when he sells his shares).

Most of these "compensation payments" do not fall within the exemption, and can cause tax problems for both the vendor and the company (which will then go for compensation from the vendor under the warranties and indemnities).

In some circumstances, these payments can be made tax free, but again this is an area for expert advice.

15.4.5. *Pre-Sale Tax Planning*

This ranges from simple things like getting cash out of the company before the sale (as most vendors are not prepared to "buy" cash in a company's bank account), through more sophisticated ideas like the ones mentioned above concerning earn-outs, to positively heroic enterprises such as moving to a tax haven for five years to escape CGT entirely (and yes, it has to be for five complete tax years, and no, it does not always work as planned).

15.4.6. *Company Purchase of Own Shares*

In some cases, rather than sell the shares to the purchaser directly, it may be possible for the company itself to buy them back from the vendor.

Bill and Ben (who are not related) own 50% each of the shares in a trading company. Bill is older than Ben, and wants to retire. Bill and Ben agree that Bill's shares are worth £200,000, but Ben cannot afford to buy him out.

The company has £100,000 cash, however, and can easily raise another £100,000 on the security of its factory, which is owned by the company.

Bill's Tax Adviser explains that provided certain conditions are fulfilled, and a "clearance" is obtained from HMRC, it will be possible for the company to buy Bill's shares from him, and for the sale to be treated as giving rise to a capital gain – (normally, if a company buys shares back from its shareholders, this is treated as if the company has paid them a dividend, which is likely to be much more expensive).

The "clearance" is obtained, and the company buys Bill's shares for £200,000. Bill pays CGT on his gain (at 10% because of entrepreneurs' relief).

The effect of the company buying these shares is that they cease to exist, and so **Ben is now the sole owner of the company**.

This special treatment is only available to a company that is trading. If the shares in a property investment company are bought back, this will be treated as if the company had paid a dividend.

15.4.7.   Timing

Capital gains tax is payable on 31 January after the end of the year of assessment in which the gain is made, so for a sale on 5 April 2018 (i.e. in 2017/18), the tax is due on 31 January 2019.

For a sale on 6 April 2018 (i.e. in 2018/19) the tax is payable a whole year later, on 31 January 2020.

Bear in mind that for CGT, a sale generally takes place on the date the contract is signed, not, if later, the day the asset is transferred to the new owner, so simply exchanging contracts on 5 April with completion at a later date will not push the sale into the next tax year.

"Options" can be used to try to "lock in" the deal, but delay it to the next tax year.

(An "option" is simply an agreement between A and B that A will sell an asset to B at a future date – a "call" option, or that B will buy the asset from A – a "put" option).

15.4.8.   Gifts to Spouse

In some circumstances, it makes sense to make a gift of some of your shares to your spouse before a sale, to use their annual exemption

(£11,700 for 20118/19 = £2,340 tax saved at 20%, plus up to another £34,500 at 10% because basic rate taxpayers pay CGT at just 10%), but there are pitfalls:

- **Entrepreneurs' relief.** You can sometimes lose entrepreneurs' relief if you gift the shares to your spouse. Check with your tax adviser before making the gift.

- **"Imperfect" gifts.** Make sure you actually do make the gift, and that you do it before the sale has been agreed, and that the spouse is included in the Sale Agreement (it is surprising how often this last point is forgotten).

  HMRC are becoming particularly hot on this point – if the gift is not properly evidenced or if the sale has already been agreed when the gift is made, HMRC will argue that all that was given was an entitlement to a proportion of the sale proceeds, and not the shares themselves. The implication is that the sale was in fact made by the original shareholding spouse.

15.4.9. Substantial Shareholding Exemption

This only applies when a company sells its shares in another company, not when an individual sells shares.

In certain circumstances, (there are numerous criteria), a company is exempt from tax on a capital gain it makes when it sells shares in another company that it owns.

The details of this relief are very complex, but if a trading company has owned more than 10% of the shares in another trading company for at least a year, and it then sells those shares, it may qualify for the exemption and not have to pay corporation tax on any gain it makes on those shares.

Of course, from the point of view of the shareholders in the vendor company, they still have to find a way to get the cash out of the company.

15.4.10. Post-Sale Tax Planning

There is much less scope for this than there is for pre-sale tax planning, which is why it is important to take tax advice **before** a sale.

15.4.11. Tax Shelters

This does not refer to "tax haven" countries, but to approved investments that offer tax deferral, such as the EIS – see section 10.2.1.

15.4.12. Losses

Losses on sales of assets in the same or an earlier tax year can be set against gains of the same tax year, so now might be the time to sell off assets that will produce a loss (but remember also that a loss must be *claimed*).

15.5. Sales of Assets and Liquidation of Company

Although it is seldom the most tax efficient way to dispose of a company, this route is often forced on the vendor because the purchaser refuses to buy the shares instead, perhaps for the reasons already explained earlier in this section.

Once the assets of the business have been sold by the company, and it has paid the resulting corporation tax on its gains, we are left with what is sometimes known as a "cash-box" company – that is, a company whose only asset is a large bank balance. Unless the company plans to use this cash to start a new business venture, of course, the next question is how to get the cash out.

What happens next?

If the company pays the cash out to its shareholders as a dividend, they will suffer income tax at 32.5% on that dividend (assuming they are higher rate taxpayers), or even at 38.1% if the dividend takes their taxable income over £150,000.

The alternative is to wind up the company and distribute its assets to its members.

This will ideally be treated as a disposal of their shares for CGT purposes, and so they will pay CGT based on the cost of their shares.

15.6. How to Liquidate a Company

There are two ways a company can be liquidated – the formal way, and the informal way.

15.6.1. A Formal Liquidation

A formal liquidation must be undertaken by a specialised accountant called a "licensed insolvency practitioner".

It tends to be expensive (not least because in some circumstances a licensed insolvency practitioner can become personally liable to the company's creditors if he gets things wrong!), but it is sometimes necessary due to the nature of the company's business – ask your accountant to advise you. It may also be necessary if the company has assets of more than £25,000 – see below.

15.6.2. An Informal Liquidation

This form of liquidation is also known as **"striking-off"**. This used to be by far the commonest form of liquidation, and it goes like this:

- The company pays all its debts and collects everything owed to it.

- The company pays out all its cash to its shareholders (it is also possible for the company to transfer any assets it may have such as a property, though this is a little more complicated to arrange). The shareholders are treated as if they had sold their shares for the amount of cash or other assets they receive.

- Finally, the company applies to the Registrar of Companies to be "struck off" the Register of Companies. Once the Registrar has done this the company is dead – though, like Dracula, it can sometimes be revived if unforeseen liabilities appear.

Since March 2012 it has been possible to use this "informal" method <u>only</u> if the company's total assets at the point of striking off are less than £25,000. If more that this is to be distributed following the business' cessation, the whole amount may need to be treated as a dividend, so a formal liquidation may be preferred.

15.6.3.   Phoenix Arrangements

Many readers will be familiar with what is referred to as "phoenixing", whereby a company's shareholders may liquidate a company, and then set up a remarkably similar company a short while later, to rise from the ashes of the first. There is actually tax legislation to preserve losses when this happens, so that the successor company can benefit from losses made by the 'old' company (but there are rules within that legislation which seek to ensure that those losses may be transferred only if the successor company takes on at least some of the debt burden of its predecessor).

Unsurprisingly, however, HMRC takes a rather dim view of phoenix arrangements where the old company had significant PAYE, VAT or other unfulfilled tax liabilities when it died. HMRC has powers to:

- Require security deposits from businesses in relation to VAT, PAYE and NICs where it perceives a risk that it may fail to settle its liabilities in future (and the government is currently consulting on extending those powers to cover Corporation Tax and Construction Industry Scheme deductions), and/or

- In quite rare circumstances, to pursue PAYE and NICs debts from certain employees, (typically the company's directors), rather than from the employing company

Very broadly, such measures are usually considered only in circumstances where HMRC realises that a director/shareholder has previously participated in a business which failed, leaving significant debts owing to HMRC, and HMRC sees a risk that the same will happen again (although this is not a necessary precursor to either course of action).

One consequence of the government's decision to tax capital gains rather less than income, is that it now perceives risk from moneybox companies and phoenix arrangements, where a company does not distribute all of its profits as earned, and is then liquidated with significant reserves on which Entrepreneurs' Relief is claimed at only 10%, for this to happen on a "rinse and repeat" cycle every few years.

The government's response has been to amend tax law so that a capital distribution on a voluntary liquidation of a close company may later be re-categorised as an income distribution – a dividend – and then re-taxed more heavily, where a director/shareholder in that company ends up carrying on a similar activity within two years of that liquidation. The rules are complex and their application far from certain, but they do include a tax-motivated arrangements requirement, and the government has said that companies undertaking ordinary commercial transactions should not be affected.

15.7. Dying in Harness

Many businessmen take the view that their company is their pension, and as such, they have no plans to liquidate or sell. Instead, the company will pay them dividends which they will live on in their retirement.

This may be a reasonable strategy, but it is important to take account of another tax that we have not yet looked at – inheritance tax.

Perhaps appropriately, one of the final chapters of this guide deals with this.

16. Inheritance Tax and Companies

Most explanations of inheritance tax ("IHT") begin with a weak joke about "death and taxes", but it is important to realise that IHT is not only a tax on death. In a number of situations, it can be payable during your lifetime.

This guide is not the place for a detailed study of all the IHT planning techniques, but in this chapter, I want to look at some examples of how IHT interacts with property companies.

16.1. IHT – the Basics

IHT is charged on "transfers of value". The commonest "transfer of value" is a gift, but as we shall see, there are other things which, sometimes unexpectedly, are transfers of value.

When a person dies, they are charged to IHT as if they had made a transfer of value of everything they owned on the day they died. In addition, any transfers of value they made in the seven years ending on the date they died are included in the assessment of the value of their chargeable Estate on death.

IHT is charged at the following rates for 2018/19, depending on whether the transfer of value was made during a person's lifetime, or on his death:

Transfer of value	Death Rate	Lifetime Rate
0 – 325,000	0%	0%
Above 325,000	40%	20%

16.2. Nil Rate Band (NRB)

The first £325,000, which is charged at 0%, is called the Nil Rate Band ("NRB"). It is often referred to as an "exemption", but this is a misleading way to think about it, as we shall see. Each individual has his or her own NRB.

Transfers to one's spouse or civil partner *are* exempt, and do not use up the deceased's NRB. Basically, if a person leaves everything to their surviving spouse, then there will be no IHT. This used to mean that the deceased's NRB was then wasted but, since 2007, the surviving spouse also acquires any NRB that the deceased has not already used against gifts, etc., to other parties. This means that it is much easier to ensure that both NRBs available to a couple are fully utilised, and it is quite common now to see the second or surviving spouse have £650,000 (2 x NRB) available on his or her death.

16.3.   Residence Nil Rate Band (RNRB)

This is a new measure, available only on death (unlike the standard NRB, which is also available to cover chargeable lifetime transfers), available with effect from 2017/18, as follows:

- £100,000 in 2017/18
- £125,000 in 2018/19
- £150,000 in 2019/20
- £175,000 in 2020/21

It is available to cover value in the deceased's home, provided it is transferred to direct descendants (children, grandchildren, etc.). It can cover only the value in the main home, so can be wasted if the value of the deceased's interest in his home falls short of the RNRB available. Like the 'ordinary' NRB, it is available to each individual, so a couple will have one each.

It follows that, by 2020/21, a couple will potentially have up to

2 x (£325,000 + £175,000) = £1million in combined (R)NRBs.

Like the standard NRB, the RNRB is transferrable between spouses; it is possible also to transfer wealth *equivalent* to the home, rather than the property itself, if (for example) the deceased had to go into care prior to death, and the former home had been sold. However, that value equivalent to the RNRB being claimed must still be transferred to direct descendants, in order to qualify. But, simply put, it does mean that there may well be more standard NRB left over to cover other assets, such as valuable company shareholdings – so long as the home itself does not use up all of the available nil rate bands.

Aside from having to ensure that value equivalent to the RNRB being claimed passes only to direct descendants, another key difference between the RNRB and the 'normal' NRB is that the RNRB can be tapered away if the chargeable value of the deceased's estate exceeds £2million. (Note that the chargeable value is net of liabilities, such as mortgages). The taper rate is 50%, meaning that the RNRB is reduced by £1 for every £2 by which the deceased's net estate exceeds £2million.

Case Study - 35   Basic NRB

Donald is a wealthy property investor, holding shares in his property company worth £1m, together with a half-share in a palatial residence. Unfortunately, he is taken far too soon in a freak sunbed accident in 2018; his Will leaves everything, including his share in the family home, to his wife, Melissa. There is no IHT on Donald's death, because he has left everything to his spouse. She will acquire Donald's NRB and RNRB, as he has used neither.

When Melissa dies in 2022, she leaves everything (including her home) to her son, Brandon; neither Donald nor Melissa made any lifetime transfers in the 7 years prior to their deaths.

Value of shares at death	£1,200,000
Add: value of home	£1,300,000

Total	£2,500,000
Deduct NRB x 2	(650,000)
RNRB x 2 £350,000 BUT: RNRB Taper - ½ x (£2.5m - £2m) = £250,000 Residual RNRB	(100,000)
Taxable	1,750,000
IHT Payable (40%)	**700,000**

IHT calculations are almost invariably far more complicated than the above example, but it serves to illustrate the basics maths of the NRB and RNRB. Melissa does not acquire Donald's NRB and RNRB that applied on his death, but his unused proportion (in this case 100%) of the Bands that apply when she later dies.

16.4. PETs

Not all transfers of value attract IHT when they are made. A simple gift from one individual, during his or her lifetime, to another will be a "potentially exempt transfer" ("PET"). This means that if the individual making the gift lives for another seven years after making it, it will fall out of account and no IHT will be charged on it when the individual dies. If, however, they die within seven years, it will form part of their estate at death.

Case Study - 36   A Failed PET

Joe is a middle aged widower. On 1 April 2017, he makes a cash gift to his son of £100,000, to help him buy a house. This is a PET for IHT purposes, and so there is no IHT to pay at the time. Sadly, during 2018, Joe is killed in a car crash. His estate at death, after deducting all debts, is worth £250,000.

Because Joe has not survived for seven years after making the gift to his son, the PET is added to his estate when calculating the IHT:

Value of estate at death	250,000
Add gifts in last seven years	100,000

Total	350,000	
Deduct NRB	(325,000)	
Chargeable to IHT at 40%	25,000	

16.5. Gift with Reservation of Benefit

A gift is only a PET if it is really given away. If the person making the gift continues to enjoy a benefit from it, it will be a **"gift with reservation of benefit. ("GWROB")**. It will still be treated as owned by the giver. The commonest example of a GWROB is where a parent gifts their house to their child, but continues to live there; however, any gift that the giver continues to enjoy will be a GWROB:

Case Study - 37   GWROB

Sue is a widow, getting on in years, and like many otherwise modestly-off people, she has one hugely valuable asset – her house. It is worth £350,000, and the mortgage was paid off long ago. The rest of her assets come to £200,000.

She makes a gift of the house to her two children, but continues to live in it. Ten years later she dies, still living in the house.

Because she "reserved a benefit" in the house, by continuing to live in it, for IHT purposes she is treated as if she still owned the house, so the value of her death estate includes the value of the house at the time of her death. It is irrelevant that she has survived for over seven years since she gave the house away – for IHT purposes it is still hers.

The GWROB rules were sometimes easy to get around, despite numerous tweaks to the legislation over the years. New rules were introduced around a decade ago, that tried to encompass GWROB scenarios. The effect of the relatively new "Pre-Owned Assets Tax" regime is that, if for some reason you are able to circumvent the GWROB regime, then you should – usually, but not always – be subjected to an annual Income Tax charge, broadly based on the rental value of any asset that you continue to enjoy, having legally given it away. The rules for "GWROB" and "POAT" can be complex, particularly in their interaction with each other, and will happily catch innocent transactions where no avoidance was intended or realised. If you think that the rules may apply, then you should get advice.

16.6. Spouse Exemption

A gift or a legacy from one spouse or civil partner to the other is exempt from IHT. If you die and leave everything absolutely to your spouse, there will be no IHT to pay, and when they die, they can use double the nil rate band at the time of their death: both theirs and yours (because you have not used yours if you leave everything to your spouse)

16.7. Business Property Relief

For IHT purposes, "business property" gets relief at either 50% or 100%, depending on its nature. The crucial types of business property for property investors are:

- An interest in a business (that is, a sole trader, or a partner)

- Shares in an unlisted **trading** company

Both these can qualify for 100% BPR, and thus effectively be exempt from IHT, but it is crucial to bear in mind that a "business" or a "trading company" does **NOT** in this context include a business that substantively involves:

- Making or holding investments – and HMRC regard property letting as falling into this category

- Dealing in land – although a property development company **may** qualify as long as it is predominantly "developing" property – new builds or major refurbishments – and not simply buying and selling properties

Most property investment companies, therefore, are unlikely to qualify for Business Property Relief, and so the planning for them will tend to involve making gifts during the owner's lifetime, and hoping to survive the necessary seven years.

This guide is not the place to look at the various planning strategies to minimise IHT – this is a huge subject, and there is probably no area of taxation where skilled professional advice is more ESSENTIAL to avoid pitfalls.

Caution

It is not an exaggeration to say that any layman who attempts to do IHT planning more sophisticated than leaving everything to his (or her) spouse is likely to produce unexpected and expensive results for himself and his family.

Even leaving everything to your spouse or civil partner could be a mistake.

16.8. Close Companies and IHT

IHT is essentially a tax on individuals (and Trusts), and there is a common misconception that it cannot apply to companies. This is generally the case, but there are exceptions:

Case Study - 38   Transfer of Value by a Close Company

Mr Smart is a widower and the sole owner of a property investment company. The value of his 100 £1 shares is £1 million. Mindful of the IHT consequences if he dies still owning all of it (no BPR, so fully chargeable to IHT), he wants to give half the company to his son (who is not involved with the company, having a full time job of his own).

He knows that if he simply gifts 50 shares to his son, he will be treated as having sold them for market value and will pay CGT on £500,000, so he comes up with another idea – he gets his son to subscribe for 100 new shares, paying their face value of £1 each.

Unfortunately, this is one of those rare examples where a close company can be involved in a transfer of value for IHT.

Because his son paid much less than market value for the shares, the shareholders before the shares were issued (here, Mr Smart) are treated as having made a transfer of value for IHT – and this type of transfer is not a gift from one individual to another, so it cannot be a PET.

It is immediately chargeable to IHT at the lifetime rate of 20%.

The amount of the transfer is the amount by which Mr Smart's estate has reduced in value, not the amount received by his son, so it is not £499,900 (the difference between the value of the shares and the amount he paid the company for them). Instead, we look at Mr Smart:

The value of each share before the issue to his son was £10,000 (1,000,000 divided by 100).

After the share issue, Mr Smart no longer has absolute control of the company, because he only has half the shares and cannot outvote his son if there is a dispute.

It is normal to discount the value of the shares by around 20% (it would have been more for a trading company) to reflect the fact that the shareholder has less than absolute control over the underlying assets in the company.

The value of Mr Smart's 100 shares is therefore £500,000 (half the value of the whole company), less £100,000 (20% discount for loss of control of his company), so his shares are now worth £400,000. His transfer of value is therefore:

Value of 100 shares (100% of company) before share issue	1,000,000
Less value of 100 shares (now just 50% of company) after share issue	(400,000)
Deemed transfer of value	600,000
Less NRB	(325,000)
Chargeable to IHT at 20% (lifetime rate)	275,000
IHT payable	55,000

> *Note – because of the way IHT is calculated on transfers like this, the actual amount might be somewhat different, but for simplicity, £55,000 gives a good idea of the amount due.*
>
> This is a rude introduction to one of IHT's most important 'lessons': it is not the value of the asset transferred that is important so much as the effect it has on your estate: giving away even a small shareholding in a company – where it means you lose a controlling majority interest – can mean a big IHT bill. Mr. Smart can console himself that he is by no means the first taxpayer – or adviser – to fall foul of this key principle.
>
> It does not end there – there is anti-avoidance legislation for CGT, which means that Mr Smart is treated as having made a disposal for CGT purposes of £500,000, by "value shifting".
>
> Fortunately for him, however, because the transfer was immediately chargeable to IHT, he can "hold over" this gain, in much the same way as he could have done if the shares had been shares in a trading company.

The above example was a disaster for Mr Smart, because he did not realise the IHT he would have to pay, but in fact much IHT planning for property investment companies revolves around deliberately incurring IHT "charges" (but usually, carefully kept within the £325,000 nil rate band so as not to have to actually pay any IHT) as a way of holding over the capital gain on a gift of the shares.

We do not want you to get lost in the detail on IHT planning for property companies – it really is a case of "don't try this at home" – but we hope you will realise from the above that IHT cannot be ignored by owners of property companies, even though they may not be around when the time comes to pay the tax!

To end on a piece of good news – IHT is normally payable (broadly) six months after the transfer of value (or the date of death), but where it is charged on property deriving its value from land, it is often possible to arrange to pay the tax in ten annual instalments – the idea being that the property need not be sold off to pay the IHT.

Good Advisors Do Save You TAX!

This section has been written by Amer Siddiq, founder of www.property-tax-portal.co.uk.

17. Finding an Accountant

There is a saying, "a good accountant pays for him/herself". Never a truer word has been spoken.

In this chapter we will become familiar with and understand how to acquire the services of an excellent accountant.

17.1. Accountants Qualifications

The first step is to ensure that your accountant is a member of a recognised institute.

Some of the popular ones amongst accountants are ACA, ACCA, ICAEW, ICAS etc.

Here is what these abbreviations stand for:

- Association of Chartered Accountants (ACA)
- Association of Chartered Certified Accountants (ACCA)
- Institute of Chartered Accountants in England and Wales (ICAEW)
- Institute of Chartered Accountants in Scotland (ICAS)

Furthermore, it would not be a bad idea to pick an accountant who is a member of the Chartered Institute of Taxation or Association of Taxation Technicians.

Getting to know the history of your proposed accountant is a very good idea, so look for the following signs:

a) Are they a former Tax Inspector?
b) Have they passed the Taxation (ATII/CTA, ATT) exams?

A qualified tax advisor is useful for all sorts of tax related services and these include:

- Preparing tax returns
- Sole trader tax returns
- Tax planning advice

It is most likely that your tax advisor will charge on an hourly basis. However, some will agree a flat fee beforehand.

It is pertinent to ask whether one should go for a general or specialist tax advisor, although it may seem better to go with the general advisor as he/she will most definitely be cheaper.

However, in the long-term the specialist may save you money because of his/her in depth knowledge and experience.

17.2. General Advisor or Tax Specialist?

A specialist will have the answer, usually to hand, whereas a non-specialist may have to consult HMRC documentation or may indeed consult the specialist and then pass the charge back on to you.

Cost can be a significant issue, as a specialist can charge around £270 per hour. For this you get about 15 minutes of quizzing followed by 45 minutes' worth of (in most cases) written response (Oh and that's plus VAT!)

To put that into perspective a non-specialist can charge around £150 per hour. A typical session with a non-specialist can take up to 2.5 hours. This time would be typically spent in the following way:

- 15 minutes of clarification.
- 1.5 hours of research.
- 45 minutes of written response.

As you can see sometimes it is beneficial if you go direct to a specialist, particularly if your questions to your accountant require him/her to study before responding.

With the above two examples in mind it is important to ascertain a working relationship with your advisor. You should be familiar with his/her area of expertise and know what their limitations are i.e. what they are not too hot on.

17.3. How to Choose Your Adviser

Before you sign up with a tax adviser or accountant, be sure to address the following:

17.3.1.   Will I Need a Tax Adviser or an Accountant?

More often than not people will actually require both, however, it is important to establish why you need them - do you need someone to manage your accounts and help you with your tax return, or someone to give you sound advice that will legally save you money. Your accountant can manage your accounts, provide compliance work, and some may even do tax planning.

However, tax advisers tend to focus solely on tax planning. They spend significant amounts of time keeping up-to-date with the latest tax legislation and tax cases to help make sure they provide their clients with great strategies that will help to reduce or eliminate tax - some of which your accountant may not even be aware of!

If we compare the accountancy profession with medicine, an accountant is the equivalent of a GP, and most of the time a GP is all you need for routine health care, but if you get seriously ill (compare with a dispute with HM Revenue and Customs) or you need surgery (tax planning), then you need a specialist consultant (a Tax Adviser).

17.3.2.   What Qualifications?

As a client you want to be assured that your tax adviser / accountant is acting in both your best interest and within the law, which is why it is important to know what qualifications your tax adviser or accountant has, and when they were achieved and if they are relevant to you. Check that the qualifications they have cover the area of taxation or accounting that you require assistance with.

17.3.3. How Much Experience do they Have?

When choosing a tax adviser or accountant, it is good to know just how much experience they have and what their reputation is.

Do not be afraid to ask how long have they been giving advice, where they worked before or if they have ever done any public speaking or written work that you can refer back to? Another good question to ask is how many existing clients they have within the area that you are interested in, for example – if you develop property, how many other developers have they provided advice for and will they be able to provide references?

Good advisers will boast about their success, so give them to the opportunity to do so!

17.3.4. How Much Will It Cost?

That really does depend on what type of advice or service you require. The fees generally reflect the adviser's / accountant's level of experience and qualifications, along with the amount of time they may have to spend on your case; in this instance you can request an estimate of the total. Also ask when fees need to be paid by.

Some accountants and tax advisers do offer 'fixed fees' for certain types of advice or help so that you know exactly what you are paying and exactly what you will receive.

Try to negotiate a fixed fee wherever possible, as good advisers won't be afraid to operate on this basis. It is far better than the 'let the clock run' approach, though in some cases such as a tax investigation, hourly charges are the only practical way to work.

17.3.5. Professional Bodies

There are various professional bodies that you will find tax advisers and accountants to be part of.

Anybody who claims to be able to give 'tax advice' should be a 'Chartered Tax Adviser' (CTA), which means that they will be member of the Chartered Institute of Taxation and will have taken and passed their examinations.

Qualified accountants will have Chartered Certified Accountant (ACCA or FCCA), or Chartered Accountant (CA, ACA or FCA) in their title.

17.3.6. What About Indemnity Cover?

If an adviser gives you inappropriate advice or your accountant does not manage your accounts correctly it could result in a huge financial loss for you.

Finding out at the beginning what indemnity cover a tax adviser or accountant has will mean peace of mind for you. Find out whether they are covered for loss of documents, court attendance and legal fees, breach of confidence or misuse of information to suggest just a few areas. Ask who they are covered by and for how much per claim.

Knowing what protection your adviser or accountant has will protect you. You will be alarmed to learn that some advisers do not even have indemnity cover and you are well advised to stay away from such advisers. Chartered accountants and Chartered Tax Advisers are required by the rules of their professional bodies to have professional indemnity insurance.

17.3.7.   *How do I Contact My Tax Adviser / Accountant?*

It can be quite frustrating when each time you phone your tax adviser or accountant they are unavailable.

Find out in advance how to contact them and if this suits you.

If you have 'ad-hoc' questions to ask your adviser or accountant and you cannot reach them, how soon will they get back to you? Also, find out if they are happy to receive email as you may prefer this method of correspondence.

Your chosen advisers should personally respond to your enquiries and calls within an agreed timescale.

A recent development has been the growth of online accountants and tax advisers, and if you do not feel the need for face to face contact with your adviser, you may want to consider using such a firm. Having lower overheads in the form of offices and meeting rooms, they are often able to offer lower fees than the conventional firms.

17.3.8.   *Keep up to Date with Tax Legislation Changes*

Tax legislation is constantly changing. That is why it is important that your adviser or accountant keeps up-to-date with all the changes.

Also, to retain their qualifications, tax advisers and accountants must adhere to on-going training programmes enforced by their regulatory bodies, to ensure that they are keeping abreast of the latest changes in legislation and the latest tax planning opportunities.

For example, CPD (Continuing Professional Development) is the compulsory training a Chartered Tax Adviser is required to do each year in order to keep his qualifications. He or she must do a minimum of 90 hours training per year; broken down into at least 20 hours "structured" training - that is, attending seminars, lectures, etc., and 70 hours "unstructured" training (such as reading textbooks and technical articles)

17.3.9. What if I Have an Emergency?

You are now aware of how to contact your tax adviser or accountant, but what happens if you have an emergency and need urgent tax advice?

How available are they in a crisis?

Knowing that you can rely on the tax adviser or accountant is an important point when considering their services. Make sure that you are able to contact them without having to arrange a formal meeting!

17.3.10. Does the Adviser Sell 'Off the Shelf' Packages?

This is a very important question to ask your adviser. There are certain advisers out there who sell tax schemes (also known as 'off the shelf' tax solutions) and earn significant amounts of commission by doing so.

"Tax Schemes" come in all sorts of forms – one example (now stopped by legislation) was the creation of artificial capital losses to set against capital gains.

 If your adviser mentions such schemes to you, then be cautious as HM Revenue and Customs are getting tough on such schemes, and legislation has been introduced requiring those using them to disclose the fact to HMRC.

18. The Importance of Tax Planning

This section has been written by Amer Siddiq, founder of www.property-tax-portal.co.uk.

We all instinctively do some tax planning in our daily lives, even if it is simply remembering to buy our "duty frees" when we return from our holiday abroad.

If you are going to make the best of your property business, then you need to be alert to the tax implications of your business plans, and to any opportunities to reduce the likely tax bill. Your instinct may be enough for your duty free goodies, but for tax on your business, you need a more structured approach!

"Tax planning" means arranging your business affairs so that you pay the minimum amount of tax that the law requires. It does not mean trying to conceal things from the Taxman, and it does not mean indulging in highly complex (and expensive!) artificial "tax avoidance" schemes.

"Every man is entitled if he can to order his affairs so that the tax attaching under the appropriate Acts is less than it would otherwise be." That is what the House of Lords said in 1935, when they found for the Duke of Westminster and against the Inland Revenue. This still holds true today, though there is now a mass of "anti-avoidance" legislation to consider when thinking about tax planning – and before you ask, the Duke's tax planning idea was stopped by anti-avoidance legislation!

18.1. Knowing When to Consider Planning

A question you will most certainly ask yourself is "when should I consider tax planning for my property business?"

The short answer is "all the time", but to be realistic, no-one is likely to do this. The trick is to develop by experience, a sense of when a tax planning opportunity (or a potentially expensive tax pitfall) is likely to present itself.

You should consider tax planning in all of the following situations, for example:

18.1.1. Buying

If you are buying a property, you need to consider:

- Buying the property – It could be you as an individual, you and your spouse, you and a business partner, a Limited Company owned by you, or perhaps a Trust you have set up. Your decision will depend on your future business strategy

- Financing the property – You will need to consider whether you are taking out a mortgage, and if so how will it be secured. It may not always make sense to secure the loan on the property you are buying if you have other assets on which you can secure the loan.

- Plans for the property – It could be that you are you buying the property to sell it again in the short term, or to hold it long term and benefit from the rental income. The tax treatment will be different according to which is the case, and different planning should be done before the property is bought.

18.1.2.   Repairs and Refurbishment

If you spend money on a property, you need to consider:

- Whether you doing it in order to sell it again in the short term, or whether you will continue letting it.

- If the work being done is classed as a **repair** to the property, or an **improvement.** See icon below for the difference between the two.

    The distinction between a repair and an improvement to a property is very important, because although the cost of repairs can be deducted from your rental income for tax purposes, an improvement can only be claimed as a deduction against CGT when you sell the property.

    Essentially, a repair is when you replace like with like, whereas an improvement involves adding to the property (say, a conservatory or a loft conversion), or replacing something with something significantly better (say, removing the old storage heaters and installing oil-fired central heating).

    HMRC do not always behave logically when it comes to repairs versus improvements.

    A taxpayer sold a seaside property, in circumstances where he would have to pay CGT on the sale profit. He had spent a lot of money on this property, which when he bought it had not been touched since the early 1950s.

    He had ripped out the old "utility" kitchen, for example, and replaced it with a state-of-the-art designer affair in gleaming slate, chrome and steel. The old 1950s cooker had had some Bakelite knobs to turn the gas on and off – the new kitchen range had the computer power of the average 1970s space capsule.

    Clearly an improvement, and so deductible from his capital gain, but HMRC tried to argue that one kitchen is much like another and he was just replacing like with like – so they said it was a repair, which was no good to him in his case as there was no rental income from which he could deduct the cost of repairs.

18.1.3.   Selling

When you decide to dispose of a property, there are other tax issues to consider:

- Who is the property going to? – If it is to someone "connected" with you, such as a close relative or a business partner, and if you do not charge them the full market value, HMRC can step in and tax you as if you had sold it for full value.

- Will you be paying CGT or income tax on the profit you make? – The planning opportunities are very different, depending on which tax is involved.

- What are the terms of the sale? Is it just a cash sale, or is the buyer a developer who is offering you a "slice of the action" in the form of a share of the profits from the development? There is important anti-avoidance legislation to consider if this is the case.

18.1.4. *Life changes*

Whenever your life undergoes some significant changes, you should consider tax planning.

Here are some examples when tax planning should be considered:

- Getting married – a married couple (and a civil partnership) have a number of tax planning opportunities denied to single people, but there are also one or two pitfalls to watch out for.

  - Moving house – it is usually not a good idea to sell the old house immediately, as there are often tax advantages to keeping it and letting it out.

  - Changing your job. You may become a higher or lower rate tax payer and this may mean you should change your tax strategy.

    If you are moving house, and you sell the old residence, you will have the cash left after you have paid off the mortgage and the various removal costs to spend on your new home. If you need a mortgage to buy the new home, the interest on that mortgage is not allowed as a deduction for tax purposes.

    If, instead, you re-mortgage the old house and let it out, ALL of the mortgage interest you pay can be deducted against the rent you receive whatever you do with the cash you have released – and you may well be able to sell the house after three years of letting (or sometimes a longer period), and pay no CGT on the increased value since you stopped living there.

  - Death – IHT is charged at 40% on the value of your estate when you die, to the extent that the value is greater than (for 2016/17) £325,000. By planning early enough it is possible to reduce the IHT burden considerably.

18.1.5. *Politics*

There are two occasions each year when you need to be particularly alert – the Pre Budget Report in November or December, and The Budget in March or April.

On both these occasions the Chancellor of the Exchequer announces tax rates, and new tax legislation, which might well affect you and your property business. In some cases, however, new tax legislation is announced at other times – it pays to keep a weather eye on the financial pages of the newspaper, or to subscribe to a magazine or journal that will alert you to important tax changes that may affect your business.

18.1.6. *End and Start of Tax Year*

The tax year ends on the 5th April each year and it is a good idea to review your tax situation before this date to make sure you are not missing any planning opportunities.

18.2. The Real Benefits of Tax Planning

Robert Kiyosaki, author of the number one bestselling book 'Rich Dad Poor Dad', says *'Every time people try to punish the rich, the rich don't simply comply, they react. They have the money, power and intent to change things. They do not sit there and voluntarily pay more taxes. They search for ways to minimize their tax burden'*
The whole purpose of tax planning is to save you tax and to put more profits in your pocket. That is why the rich are always looking at ways of beating the taxman, because they benefit from tax planning.

18.2.1. *Paying Less Tax*

Don't fall into the trap where you only think about tax when you are considering selling or even worse after you have sold the property.

By taking tax advice at the right times and on a regular basis you will legitimately avoid or reduce taxes both in the short and the long term.

This means that you will have greater profits to spend as you wish.

18.2.2. *Clear 'Entrance' and 'Exit' Strategies*

When you sit down and analyse properties that you are considering for investment, you will no doubt look at how much rental income the property will generate and what you expect to achieve in capital appreciation.

Knowing the estimated tax liabilities right from the outset will save you from any nasty surprises in the future.

> Your personal circumstances can change at a whim. The last thing that you want to do is fall into a situation where you are forced to sell a property but are unable to pay the taxman because you never considered your tax situation.

18.2.3. *Staying Focused*

When you are deciding on the property investment strategies that you are going to adopt it is a good idea to talk them through with a tax adviser.

If your investment strategy changes then it is likely to have an impact on your tax strategy, so it should be reviewed with your tax adviser.

Your tax strategy will go hand in hand with your investment strategy and will help you to keep focused on your property investment and financial goals.

18.2.4. *Improving Cash Flow*

One of the challenges that you will face as a property investor is cash flow. In other words, you need to make sure that you have enough money coming in from your property business to pay for all property related bills, maintenance and repairs, and of course tax on the rental profits.

> Remember, timing of expenditures can be the difference between a 'high' and a 'nil' tax bill. Therefore, keeping in regular contact with your tax adviser, especially when coming towards the end of the tax year, can have a significant impact on your property cash flow.

18.2.5.   *Avoiding Common Tax Traps*

There are many tax traps that you can fall into if you have not taken any tax advice at all, not to mention the numerous great tax planning opportunities you will miss out on too.

It is not uncommon to hear stories about investors who have made a £100,000 profit on a single property and then sold it without taking any tax advice whatsoever. If you fall into this situation, then you could be facing a tax bill of up to £28,000.

It will hurt you even more if after selling you realise that you could have easily turned the tax liability to zero had you taken some simple tax advice.

Good tax advisers will know of the most common traps that you are likely to fall into, so a few minutes spent wisely could save you thousands in taxes.

18.3. The Golden Tax Rules

The challenge to you as a property investor will no doubt be how to grow a profitable portfolio. One of the easiest ways you can make money in property is to pay less tax.

18.3.1.   *Education…Education…Education*

Whether you are starting out in property investing or are an experienced landlord with a sizeable portfolio, there is one thing that you should always do - educate yourself to make sure you are:

a) complying with the ever changing legal requirements

b) learning how to make your investments more profitable

c) making sure you keep up-to-date with tax changes that may affect your tax liability.

Although there is never a substitute for taking professional advice, you should keep yourself updated so that you can discuss these opportunities with your adviser at your next appointment.

18.3.2.   *Prevention is Better Than Cure*

There is a proverb 'prevention is better than cure' (believe it or not this was first said by the famous medieval philosopher Erasmus) and he probably was not thinking about tax when he said it, but it most certainly applies.

Planning for a tax situation you are likely to face is much better than trying to get out of a tax problem that you have unknowingly (or even knowingly) fallen into. It is certain that trying to get out of a tax problem will cost much more in specialist/consultancy fees and there is never a guarantee that you will get out of the problem.

Congratulations – You've now finished 'Tax DOs and DON'Ts for Property Companies'

To learn even more ways on how to legitimately cut your property tax bills please visit: www.property-tax-portal.co.uk.

Special Bonus Report

Companies and Overseas Property Investment

By Daniel Feingold

19. International and Offshore Companies by Daniel Feingold

So far in this guide we have looked at UK Companies for UK property investments.

However, a growing number of people are now investing overseas. Whenever this happens investors are never sure which type of structure to use for such investments.

In this chapter International and Offshore tax specialist, Daniel Feingold, goes through the different options that are available.

19.1. About Daniel Feingold

Daniel is a Barrister who heads Strategic Tax Planning, a Firm of Tax Lawyers that has as one of its specialities UK and International Tax Planning for both high net worth individuals and corporate clients. This includes both structuring for UK clients investing in property abroad and UK property acquisitions for foreign investors. His advice is sought after by many accounting and law firms around the UK and overseas.

Daniel has over 32 years' experience specialising in tax law since qualifying as a Barrister in July 1983.

He has spent time at the Bar, in several leading City of London law firms and in the International Tax Department of a leading accountancy firm, before establishing his own Firm of Tax Lawyers.

Daniel is the lead international tax expert and a technical author for www.property-tax-portal.co.uk.

Daniel has written and lectured extensively on property tax planning; including the pitfalls of Spanish and French property investment and is a regular contributor to several publications on the whole spectrum of tax planning, especially avoiding capital gains on property sales.

Daniel is known as a 'creative' tax expert and has formulated his own unique tax mitigating solutions.

You can learn more about Daniel on-line at the following link:

→ www.property-tax-portal.co.uk/consultancy_daniel.shtml

19.2. Watch Out for the Single Solution Approach

The first and most important point to understand when considering overseas property investments is that one single solution will not fit all investment scenarios. This is regardless of what any advisor may tell you.

This is something that is very important (in fact critical) to understand.

You are likely to need an individual solution to fit around your specific circumstances and that is the key to successful tax planning in this area.

A solution that works for one person might actually trigger a huge extra UK tax liability for another.

19.3. Using an Offshore Company

One of the most popular solutions that are recommended time and time again for people who are investing in overseas property is to purchase the property through an Offshore Company.

This Offshore Company could be situated in a country such as Jersey, Gibraltar, the Isle of Man, or in fact, any well-known offshore tax haven.

The advisors who recommend such a structure usually claim that simply using such a Company will avoid the following taxes:

- local capital gains tax

- reduce or eliminate local income tax

- local inheritance laws and taxes

- wealth taxes.

It is important to understand that most of these claims are not true!

19.4. The SEVEN pitfalls of using an Offshore Company

Below you will find the most common found issues with setting up and using an Offshore Company.

Income Tax on Rental Income
The one tax that the use of an Offshore Company will not reduce at all is the income tax on rental income.

This means that if the Company that you have set-up receives rental income from your properties then local tax will be due on this.

Withholding Tax
It is also important to understand that most countries have what is called a withholding tax on rental income.

The agent or the tenant is normally obliged to deduct this tax and pay it over to the local tax authority. In practice, withholding is not made by the agent or tenant and the property owner has to pay the withholding tax over to the local tax authorities when filing their annual local tax return.

Another type of withholding tax is usually due when you sell your property.

The property purchaser is obliged to withhold between 3% or 15% of the purchase price. This is handed directly over to the tax authorities in the country where the property is situated by the purchaser.

Examples of this include Spain, where the purchaser must withhold 3% of the purchase price, and the US, where the purchaser must withhold 15% of the purchase price.

In both situations the only way to get the money back (if your capital gains tax liability there is less), is to file a local tax return.

Offshore Companies do not avoid withholding taxes either on income or capital gains.

The other factor that is often missing in the advice that people are getting in these standard solutions is the UK tax perspective.

Offshore Companies can sometimes avoid local Inheritance taxes, but this is not universal.

The one tax they are usually good at avoiding is local wealth taxes, because these are applied only to individuals.

However the cost or running an Offshore Company is often as much as the annual wealth taxes!

Don't forget the UK Tax Perspective
It is all very well if your Company can avoid local taxes supposedly, but you need to understand the UK tax law as well.

Offshore Companies can create many UK tax problems – remember this!

There has been a long history of attack by HMRC on the use of Offshore Companies. After all, if it was so simple to use Offshore Companies, then the use of onshore local standard UK Companies wouldn't be such a regular occurrence!

The Anti-Avoidance Rule
When using an Offshore Company, it is also vital to understand that there is an anti-avoidance provision, which is now called section 720 of the Income Taxes Act 2007 Act of 1988.

This is an anti-avoidance rule going back to 1936.

The objective of the rule is basically to look through any transaction where a person transfers their rights or their money to a person based outside the UK.

This can involve the transferring of rights or money to a Company, trust or an individual with the objective of avoiding UK income tax.

This means that even if you set up an Offshore Company, then the rental income that is coming through that Offshore Company could still be taxable on you in the UK using this anti-avoidance rule and therefore be subject to UK income tax.

The only new development is that if the Company and the underlying property are within the EU and preferably in the same country, the rules may no longer apply. This needs specialist advice.

In other words, the Offshore Company will have no effect whatsoever for UK income tax purposes.

Charging of Capital Gains to Shareholder
There is also a parallel provision for capital gains tax that is section 13 of the Taxation of Chargeable Gains Act 1992.

This provision creates a "look through" if an Offshore Company sells a property for instance, and realizes a capital gain, and a UK shareholder has more than a 25% interest in that Company. The test takes into account any shares held by "connected persons" such as parents and grandparents, children, sisters and brothers and business partners.

The legislation will attribute a corresponding proportion of the capital gain the Company makes to that individual. In other words, a "look-through".

Even if you simply put the shares in the name of your wife and your children, it will not work because the legislation will "look-through" that and charge the tax on you.

Every UK resident shareholder will end up getting a tax bill when the Offshore Company sells the property. The effect is there will be no tax benefits whatsoever for UK capital gains tax purposes from using an Offshore Company.

There is a new exemption for overseas property held by a Company and used as part of a Furnished Holiday Lettings business ("FHL").

Benefits in Kind (BIK)
Another very real problem is a tax charge based on the use of the property as a benefit in kind.

If you own your own UK Company then you may well already be familiar with this.

If the Company provides you with a car then you pay tax based on the type of car that is provided by the Company. This is a benefit in kind. If the Company pays for the petrol that you use in the car, then again it is a benefit in kind and you are taxed on this.

The same thing happens with a property, if that property is used for your benefit.

If the property is a pure investment property and you rent it out then it is not a problem as you are not receiving any personal benefit from the property.

If you have an Offshore Company that is holding a single property which you use as a holiday home then this will under Section 45 Of the Finance Act 2008 **NOT BE** treated as a benefit in kind and you will **NOT BE** liable to pay tax on this benefit. The rules are very restrictive. The Company must only be a Company that just holds a single Foreign Holiday home and does not have any other activities. If you have a Company with more than one property, or one that has other activities, then you will have to pay tax on the benefit at your highest income tax rate.

Say that you own a holiday home through an Offshore Company in Portugal and you also have an investment in a Portuguese ice cream parlour and three other rental properties in that same Company. In the summer months of August the rental income generated by this property would be approximately £2,000 per week.

Instead of letting the property out you decide to use it for a family holiday for two weeks. If you don't pay the Company £4,000 then you could end up with tax bill of 45% on the £4,000. In certain circumstances, the benefit in kind charge can be higher than this, based on when the property is "available" (that is, not let to a third party), rather than when you actually occupy it.

Now it is not quite as simple as that, because the Company also has to pay UK national insurance contributions at 13.8% on the benefit that you have received. If HMRC discover such a structure not declared to them and ask about personal use they may argue that it has been available all year to the tax payer. If the owner rents it out for some of the time and pays the BIK of his own accord on an ongoing basis, then this is unlikely to be raised. Even if it is raised HMRC will accept personal time use based on evidence. However, if there is no evidence then there will be a problem.

Here is a summary of the Section 45 Finance Act 2008 provisions, which will not help real investors just those with a single holiday home held in an Offshore Company. The main motivation is usually to avoid local wealth and inheritance taxes.

- The Company owning the property is itself owned by individuals
- The property is the Company's only or main asset
- The Company's only activity is the holding of the property (it appears this exemption will only apply to one property)
- The acquisition of the property was not financed by a connected Company
- No improvements were paid for by a connected Company

Central Management & Control
Another very common and key problem with Offshore Companies is a concept of English tax law that is known as **central management and control**.

This is an approach that the HMRC are using more and more.

If an Offshore Company only has UK directors and it is run from the UK then HMRC will argue that the Company's residence is actually in the UK for tax purposes. This is because its central management and control is in the UK and therefore it should be taxed like a UK Company.

This means that if the Company receives rental income then it will be charged to UK corporation tax.

There has been a case on this issue of Company residence, the "Wood and another v Holden" case, which was decided on 26 January 2006 in the Court of Appeal in favour of the taxpayer. The HMRC were refused leave to appeal the case to the House of Lords. Then HMRC had a victory in another Case on Company residence that indicates it will be very hard to prove central management & control outside the UK. That case is Laerstate BV v Revenue & Customs [2009]. This was a First-Tier Tribunal case but due to the death of the owner was never appealed, but does not have the same value as the *Wood v Holden* case.

The basis of this ruling shows that unless a Company is genuinely run from abroad then it will not be resident in the UK, but the strategies used by the Company to achieve this are unlikely to be practical for the average property investor due to the costs of doing so.

How to Avoid the Issue of Central Management & Control
In order for the problem of central management and control in the UK to be successfully avoided, the Company would have to be run by directors who were not resident in the UK. These directors would then have to hold board meetings and make decisions about the Company – and not just "rubber stamp" decisions made by the shareholders in the UK.

In other words, the Company is genuinely going to have to be run outside the UK, presumably in the tax haven where it has been incorporated.

The real result of this is that it makes it very costly to operate an Offshore Company and another practical problem is that the investor loses direct control of his property investments because every time he wants to make a decision, he has to put that decision to the Board of Directors, who have to hold a meeting.

Therefore as you can imagine, it is not really very practical to achieve central management control abroad, although theoretically following the Wood and another v Holden case, it may be possible to do so.

19.5. Using Local Companies

An alternative strategy to using an Offshore Company is to use a local Company in the place where the property is being purchased.

Now, sometimes there is a real need for this method in places such as Bulgaria, where until recently it was not possible for foreigners to own freehold Bulgarian property.

The only way to overcome this was to form a Bulgarian registered Company, which could then hold the property.

Sometimes when you form a local Company it can avoid the withholding tax rules on rental income and also reduce the amount of capital gains tax. However, although this is possible, in practice, it is not very common.

Challenges faced when using a Local Company
Mostly local Companies are taxed in a fairly similar way to any other individual holding property.

This means that once again you have got similar problems to running any Offshore Company from a UK perspective, as a result of the section 720 Income Taxes Act problems.

There is however a defence to this, which is to demonstrate that there was no tax avoidance motive. Add to this a Defence based on EU law. A provision that allows you to move your money and invest it anywhere in the EU without prejudice. In other words, the reason for setting up the Company was purely to comply with local property laws such as in the Bulgarian situation. If you can demonstrate this to HMRC then it is possible that there will not be a problem with rental income held within the Company. (This has been bolstered by changes in the Finance Bill 2013, which place in law the EU provisions).

However, it may be very costly in terms of professional fees, (if HMRC takes up this point) to prove to them that your motive was not a tax avoidance one. This defence has been successfully raised and saved people substantial amounts of tax, interest and penalties being recovered by HMRC, but only after professional action.

The other issue you need to overcome is section 13 of the Taxation of Chargeable Gains Act 1992, as mentioned earlier. You also have to consider the impact of Brexit which may or may not remove the EU defence against Section 720, Income Taxes Act.

19.6. Using a Double Tax Treaty to Your Advantage

Many of the double tax treaties between the UK and various other countries, for instance Bulgaria, Spain etc., will give one country sole taxing rights to a Company's profits if a Company is resident in that country.

In other words, the income passing through a local Company holding investment property could possibly trigger tax under section 720 Income Taxes Act. The position on Section 720 and whether a treaty can protect against it is unclear! (This has been clarified in Finance Act 2013). That if taxing the income would be a breach of EU Law and there is a good reason for using the local company, then S720 is not applicable buts its complicated and subject to conditions. However, the good news is that a treaty will defend against capital gains tax being attributed to shareholders with a more than 25% shareholding.

This therefore means that using a local Company could prove a good way of creating a capital gains tax deferral.

Let us look at a practical example where this may happen.

Suppose you start off by purchasing a small apartment and after a few years you make a capital gain on it and you reinvest that money into a larger villa. You will not create a UK capital gains liability at that point in the local Company if the country where it is situated has a double tax treaty with the UK with the appropriate clause giving sole taxing rights to that country. However there may be local capital gains tax on the Company.

Some countries have rules where if you reinvest the money in more property there is a deferral. This means that using a local Company for reinvesting can create a successful deferral until you sell the shares in the Company, which could be many years in the future! Contrast this with most offshore tax haven companies that have no double tax treaties!

19.7. CM&C and Local Companies

Finally, we come back to the issue of central management and control.

This can also be a problem with local Companies, just as it is with Offshore Companies.

Therefore, to get the tax benefits of capital gains deferral and possible rental income deferral you have to appoint a majority of local directors and make sure that they hold meetings. Once again, there is a cost involved in doing this and therefore it is important to weigh up the costs of having local directors and meetings against the possibility of deferring capital gains tax and income tax.

19.8. Using a UK Company to Buy Overseas Property

Another solution available for purchasing property abroad is to actually use a UK Company.

In this scenario the UK Company will be set-up and managed in the UK and purchase properties overseas.

This is a good solution, if there are no **foreign branch** tax rules locally in the country where the property is situated.

19.9. Foreign Branch Tax Rules

Foreign branch tax rules can be triggered where a Company is resident in one country, but is operating in another country. For example, you may own a UK Company and use it to buy investment properties overseas and receive rental income from them. If that other country applies this "foreign branch" rule there could be tax due in that country on the profit made by the "foreign branch".

The country where the property is owned will charge the additional tax and this can in some cases end up being a major tax burden and problem.

If this is the case then using a UK Company is not to be recommended.

Normally, however, the UK double taxation treaties such as those with Spain or Portugal will eliminate these foreign branch tax rules.

However, one place in which there is a particular problem with foreign branch tax rules is the United States. They will charge a foreign Company operating in the US taxes of up to 26%.

The corporation tax rate in the US is now 21%.

They have a foreign branch tax, which is in fact reduced under the UK/US double tax treaty to 5%. When you add those together the cumulative rate is close to 26%. This is especially so bearing in mind that a UK individual would only pay 28% capital gains tax on an investment and so using a UK Company in the US is actually a disaster! (Because a UK investor then has to extract the money from the Company and face a further 38.1% income over £150,000 on doing this by dividend.) If US capital gains tax is paid @ 15% on gains up to $400,000 and this can be credited against UK Capital gains tax @ 28%, then the UK capital gains tax is only payable @ 13%. So, using a UK Company to invest in US residential property can produce an effective combined tax rate of up to 64.1%!

19.10. Understanding Foreign Tax Rates

Another thing to check is whether the local foreign taxes are higher than the 19% UK rate (as in the US example above).

If your UK Company tax rate is going to be 19% and the foreign taxes are 26% then it is tax inefficient. Although you can set the foreign tax off against the UK tax, so you will not have to pay any UK tax, you cannot get a repayment of the foreign tax that is greater than your UK tax liability. This means that in this example you have lost 7% to foreign tax that you cannot recover.

19.11. Extracting Money from Your UK Company

We have already seen that if you pay income tax at the higher rate of 40% or the 45% rate on incomes above £150,000, you will have an additional tax liability of 32.5% or 38.1% when you extract dividends from your UK Company. This can make holding a property through a Company unattractive if the proceeds of sale are extracted by dividend, unless a basic rate taxpayer such as a non-working spouse is gifted all the shares and extracts the money. They can have dividends of up to £5,000 tax free per year and after that up to the basic rate tax band for 2017-2018 of £33,500 at 7.5% tax. This is in addition to the tax free personal allowance of £11,500. An alternative will be to liquidate the Company and pay UK Capital Gains at either 10% up to £45,000 (assuming no other income at all) and 20% above that.

19.12. Using Two Companies

A more complex tax solution that is sometimes recommended to people is to use a holding Company to hold the shares in the property owning Company. This will normally involve using both an Offshore Company and either a local or UK Company.

The objective of this strategy is to sell shares in the local Company, or more often in the top Company, which may be either a UK or an Offshore Company. In some situations this can prevent the capital gain on the sale of the shares in the property Company being attributed to the UK shareholders of the holding Company.

It is all very well for an advisor to recommend this solution, as it is good structure in certain situations and can eliminate local capital gains tax.

However, one of the problems that I have come across is that when you come to sell your property you will find very few buyers who are willing to buy shares in an Offshore or a UK Company.

They just want to buy the property itself!

I have come across numerous instances where people have bought such structures and found out there are hidden tax liabilities.

These tax liabilities are in the country where the property is situated.

For a long time there was a structure whereby there was a Spanish Company holding a property and above it was a Company located in Gibraltar. Lots of UK individuals were encouraged to use this structure as a means of avoiding Spanish capital gains and wealth taxes.

In practice, most of these structures have turned out to produce hidden tax liabilities and the use of this type of structure has ended up not only costing a lot in tax, but also in professional fees to negotiate with the authorities to agree a settlement of the tax liabilities.

Portugal was another place where such structures were immensely common. However, the Portuguese government introduced a special transfer tax at 16.25% to eliminate the advantages of such a structure. This means that anybody who is not aware of this and is offered a Portuguese property in an Offshore Company could face a large tax bill there!

Most people are now aware of this. However, if you are new to investing overseas and such a structure is offered then get proper professional advice.

I come across very few people who are prepared to take on these structures without doing extensive research and getting assurances from local advisors and UK advisors that there are no hidden liabilities.

On top of that the purchaser will want a substantial reduction in the price that they are paying for the property, just in case there are any hidden liabilities.

So the whole thing will end up being a very drawn out process and you will limit the number of potential purchasers to sell on to and you will end up taking a lower price.

So in reality, these double structure Companies are generally to be avoided for the following reasons:

- They usually come with hidden taxes

- Two Companies = two sets of costs of managing and running a Company

- Few people are prepared to take on such structures; they just want the property

- Purchasing the structure can incur high fees as the purchaser will need to consult various advisors.

19.13. Using a Nominee Company

This is a relatively new solution and can be useful in the right circumstances

The idea behind a UK nominee Company is that it acts like a trustee. In other words, it is just holding the legal title to the property for the benefit of the beneficiary.

Normally that would be the purchaser - yourself.

The idea is that this UK structure relies on the fact that the foreign tax authorities do not understand this concept of English law, where you can separate out the legal title and the beneficial ownership. In other words, the name of the person registered as owning the property can be different to the owner in law. Most European countries do not have this concept although it tends to be used in some of the Caribbean countries.

If you can use this type of Company it can be avoid local inheritance taxes, and possibly local capital gains taxes and wealth taxes.

However, it is highly specialized strategy and can only work in limited circumstances.

The idea that you can just pick one of these up off the shelf and use it to buy property anywhere would be misguided.

You need specific advice on how this is going to work for your circumstances and in the country where you are investing.

If this solution is available, then it is a relatively cheap solution to implement.

19.14. EFURBS

Finally, I want to look at a very sophisticated idea that can be used as a way to hold foreign property investment.

Following the Finance Act 2011, any payments into an EFURBS that are for the benefit of an Employee/Director will be subject to PAYE tax like ordinary wages. The Company will get a corporate tax deduction for the sums placed in the EFURBS.

It may be possible to pay in a small sum to cover the deposit and then for the EFURBS to loan the balance by mortgage.

This opens up the possibility of using an Offshore EFURBS as a holding vehicle for foreign investment property. It may need to use an Offshore Company below it to hold the property, but this is a genuine opportunity.

The way you can extract money from the EFURBS is like any other pension fund and eventually take out an annuity in the form of a guaranteed annual payment. This means you can either sell the property or take the rental income as an annual income after age 55.

Another way of actually getting money out of the EFURBS is it can actually pay you all of the money that is in the EFURBS, but you will have to suffer UK income tax at 40% or 45%.

However, by having a very long-term deferral, in other words you might not make that payment until you're 65 or 75; you have built up a huge sum of money tax-free on an ongoing basis.

If you were not UK Resident when you extracted money from the EFURBS, this could avoid any UK Tax consequences and hopefully any Tax in your new Country of residence, subject to specialist tax advice at that time.

An EFURBS is going to be quite costly to set up and there are going to be ongoing administration costs. However, for a significant investment (say £1m plus property investment overseas) and for the right client it is a very useful tax deferral vehicle and one that clients in the right circumstances should really be looking at.

There are new proposals that became law in 2017 that impact the use of such a structure in the future, so be aware of this and get specialist advice.

There may be other offshore pension vehicles, such as Qualifying Non-UK Pension Schemes (QNUPS) that can achieve the same effect of deferral and actually have Inheritance tax advantages as well, but they also need specialist advice to implement.

EFURBS/QNUPS need good specialist tax advice to make sure they will work for a property investment

19.15. A Final Word

In this chapter I have covered a number of solutions that may be proposed to you for investing overseas.

Some advisers will recommend 'off the shelf' packages to you that they will claim will mitigate taxes.

Being a specialist in Offshore and International taxation and having worked in this area for over 32 years, it is my experience that too many of these 'off the shelf packages' will not work.

Every person who is looking to invest overseas will need specific tax advice based on their personal circumstances and their investment strategy.

So before you invest overseas, make sure you consult a credible International/Offshore tax specialist and get proper written advice.

20. Appendix A – Template Documents

On the following two pages you will find template documents that you can use.

Examples of these documents are given in section 6.4.

The two documents are as follows:

- Meeting Minute
- Dividend Confirmation

Meeting Minute

Name of Company: _____
Company Registration No: _____

Address: _____

_____

_____

Minutes of a Meeting of the Board of Directors

Date of the meeting held at the Registered Office of the Company: ___/___/___

Present:

_____   _____

_____   _____

DIVIDENDS

It was resolved that the company pay an interim dividend in respect of the period ending

___/___/___ to holders registered as at ___/___/___ as follows:

Share Class	Dividend Rate	Date to be Paid
Ordinary of _____	_____ per share	___/___/___

ANY OTHER BUSINESS:

_____

_____

Signed on Behalf of the Board

Name_____   Date: ___/___/___   Position: _____

Dividend Confirmation

Name of Company: _____
Company Registration No: _____

Address: _____

_____

Dividend Confirmation

Interim dividend for the period ending ___/___/___ to shareholders registered on
___/___/___

Payment Date
___/___/___

Shareholder Details
_____
_____
_____
_____
_____
_____

Shareholding	Dividend Rate	Dividend Payment
_____Ordinary shares of_____	____ **per share**	£_____

This dividend confirmation should be kept as part of your financial records.

_____
(company secretary)
___/___/___

Date:

Appendix B – Tables

Comparing Individual Property Investor with a Company

Rental Profit	2018/19			2020/21		
	Net Income as Individual Investor	Net Income Through Company (No Interest)	Saving / (Cost) of Incorporation	Net Income as Individual Investor	Net Income Through Company (50% Interest)	Saving / (Cost) of Incorporation
-	-	-	-	-	-	-
10,000	10,000	8,886	(1,114)	10,000	8,898	(1,102)
15,000	14,370	12,936	(1,434)	14,500	13,048	(1,452)
20,000	18,370	16,751	(1,619)	18,500	16,996	(1,504)
25,000	22,370	20,497	(1,873)	22,500	20,834	(1,666)
30,000	26,370	24,243	(2,127)	26,500	24,673	(1,827)
35,000	30,370	27,990	(2,380)	30,000	28,512	(1,488)
40,000	34,370	31,736	(2,634)	32,500	32,351	(149)
45,000	38,370	35,482	(2,888)	35,000	36,189	1,189
50,000	41,640	39,228	(2,412)	37,500	40,028	2,528
55,000	44,640	42,975	(1,665)	40,000	43,867	3,867
60,000	47,640	45,962	(1,678)	42,500	47,606	5,106
70,000	53,640	51,429	(2,211)	46,500	53,209	6,709
80,000	59,640	56,897	(2,743)	48,500	58,811	10,311
90,000	65,640	62,364	(3,276)	52,500	64,414	11,914
100,000	71,640	67,832	(3,808)	57,500	70,016	12,516
110,000	75,640	73,299	(2,341)	61,750	75,619	13,869
120,000	79,640	78,767	(873)	66,000	81,189	15,189
130,000	84,900	83,245	(1,655)	70,250	85,424	15,174
140,000	90,900	86,941	(3,959)	74,500	89,159	14,659
150,000	96,900	90,586	(6,314)	78,750	92,916	14,166
160,000	102,400	95,736	(6,664)	83,000	98,519	15,519
170,000	107,900	101,203	(6,697)	87,250	104,121	16,871
180,000	113,400	106,671	(6,729)	91,500	109,724	18,224
190,000	118,900	111,876	(7,024)	95,750	114,861	19,111
200,000	124,400	116,890	(7,510)	100,000	119,999	19,999
300,000	179,400	167,029	(12,371)	142,500	171,376	28,876
400,000	234,400	217,168	(17,232)	185,000	222,753	37,753

The above table looks at the potential savings (or costs) to an unincorporated landlord running his or her residential property investment business through a company instead.

The 2018/19 tax year columns assume that the business has NO finance costs (see Chapter 5) and has to extract all of the company's profits for living expenses, rather than allowing at least some of the funds to "roll up" in the company (see Chapter 4). It clearly shows that there is no benefit to incorporation using today's rates and allowances, for a BTL investor, in such circumstances.

If, in contrast, we compare those results with figures for a similar business but in 2020/21 and where the interest accounts for 1/3rd of the rent roll, (i.e., where rental profit after interest is £50,000, the interest cost was £25,000), then the potential saving of using a corporate model soon becomes apparent. Once the taxpayer is being taxed as if he or she were a Higher Rate taxpayer, the net cost of getting only a 20% tax "credit" instead of full tax relief on one's residential mortgage interest payments starts to become increasingly punitive as net profits rise.

Note that:

- Interest costs are not fixed but are half of the net profit - £25,000 where net profits are £50,000, and £50,000 where net profits are £100,000
- The model uses the expected rates for 2020/21
- The model assumes a small salary of £8,400 (£700 per month) and the rest taken through dividends

Comparing Net Developer Income: Personal v Through a Company

Rental Profit	Net Income as Individual Developer	Net Income Through Company	Saving / (Cost) of Incorporation
-	-	-	-
10,000	9,705	8,886	(819)
15,000	13,625	12,936	(689)
20,000	17,175	16,751	(424)
25,000	20,725	20,497	(228)
30,000	24,275	24,243	(32)
35,000	27,825	27,990	165
40,000	31,375	31,736	361
45,000	34,925	35,482	557
50,000	38,000	39,228	1,228
55,000	40,900	42,975	2,075
60,000	43,800	45,962	2,162
70,000	49,600	51,429	1,829
80,000	55,400	56,897	1,497
90,000	61,200	62,364	1,164
100,000	67,000	67,832	832
110,000	70,800	73,299	2,499
120,000	74,600	78,767	4,167
130,000	79,660	83,245	3,585
140,000	85,460	86,941	1,481
150,000	91,260	90,586	(674)
160,000	96,560	95,736	(824)
170,000	101,860	101,203	(657)
180,000	107,160	106,671	(489)
190,000	112,460	111,876	(584)
200,000	117,760	116,890	(870)
300,000	170,760	167,029	(3,731)
400,000	223,760	217,168	(6,592)

The above table (using 2018/19 rates and allowances) shows that, purely in terms of net income yields, there remains some tax-based benefit for trading property developers to incorporate – within a range of profits. The model assumes that the company pays out a modest salary of £8,400 a year, and the rest of its post-tax profits as dividends.

When comparing the above two tables, the difference in outcomes between property investors and property developers is attributable to the additional National Insurance Contributions (NICs) that developers have to pay if they operate in a personal capacity. The current Chancellor seems keen to increase self-employed NICs, saying that they are too low when compared to the amount of NICs that the Treasury can enjoy from an employee on an equivalent level of income, and this is unfair on employees. (It seems to have escaped the Chancellor that most of the additional NICs are actually paid by the employee's employer, which is hardly the self-employed individual's "fault"!)

If, however, the Chancellor is ultimately successful in increasing the NICs yield from the self-employed then, ironically, this may well make incorporation more attractive, as the effective tax cost of self-employment rises in comparison, since NICs can generally be avoided in the corporate model by sticking to a low salary.

Lightning Source UK Ltd.
Milton Keynes UK
UKHW05f0653110418
320849UK00002B/5/P